Ghosts of the Past

True Paranormal Unsolved Mysteries

Rayvn Salvador

MADNESS
NEVERMORE

GHOSTS OF THE PAST: True Paranormal Unsolved Mysteries

Rayvn Salvador

eBook ISBN: 978-1-960040-10-7

ISBN: 978-1-960040-11-4

Introduction

In the vast expanse of our world, there exist realms shrouded in mystery, where the inexplicable dances with the mundane, and the ordinary gives way to the extraordinary. These enigmatic corners of existence challenge our perceptions, beckoning us to venture beyond the confines of rationality into realms of the unexplained. Welcome to a journey that delves into the heart of the paranormal, where the veil between the known and the unknown grows thin and the whispers of the supernatural echo through the corridors of time.

For centuries, humanity has been captivated by tales of the paranormal: encounters with ghosts, perplexing phenomena, and bizarre occurrences that defy all logical explanations. From ancient folklore to modern-day urban legends, these stories have woven themselves into the fabric of our collective consciousness, irrevocably changing our understanding of the world around us. Yet amid the countless accounts of the supernatural, certain mysteries stand apart—puzzles that continue to enthrall, even in the face of relentless scrutiny and investigation.

In this exploration of real-life paranormal unsolved mysteries, we embark on a quest to unravel the secrets of the unexplained. From haunted houses to UFO sightings, and cryptid encounters to inexplicable disappearances, each chapter presents a succinct and captivating case study that challenges our understanding of reality and pushes the boundaries of our imagination. As we delve deeper, we will encounter a tapestry of stories—some chilling, some perplexing, but all tantalizingly mysterious.

But why are these stories so compelling? What drives us to seek answers to questions that seem to defy all reason? Perhaps it is the inherent human desire to understand the unknown, to shine a light into the darkness and illuminate the hidden truths that lie beyond. Or maybe it is the thrill of the chase, the exhilarating pursuit of knowledge, that propels us forward on our quest for understanding. Whatever the reason, one thing is certain: The allure of the paranormal is as irresistible as it is inexorable, drawing us ever closer to the mysteries that lie just beyond our grasp.

So, dear reader, prepare yourself for a voyage into the unknown, where the line between fact and fiction blurs, and the truth remains tantalizingly out of reach. Welcome to the realm of real-life paranormal unsolved mysteries, where the only limit is our imagination, and the adventure never truly ends. Buckle up.

Chapter One

Haunted Houses and Ghostly Encounters

In this chapter, we delve into the vexing mysteries that shroud haunted houses and ghostly encounters, exploring the eerie manifestations and inexplicable phenomena that have plagued these locations for generations. From spectral apparitions to inexplicable poltergeist activity, each haunting presents a puzzle that defies all rational explanation, leaving investigators and skeptics alike grasping for answers.

Brace yourself for a unnerving journey of discovery, where the spirits of the past await to tell their tales. As we unravel the mysteries that lie within, may we uncover the truth that rests hidden in the shadows and illuminate the darkness that surrounds us.

THE AMITYVILLE HORROR HOUSE

The story of the Amityville Horror House is one that continues to captivate and terrify audiences around the world. Located in Amityville, New York, this infamous house gained notoriety in the 1970s when the Lutz family claimed to have experienced a series of terrifying and unexplainable events after moving in.

Imagine it. It's a dark, stormy night in 1974, and you stumble upon a beautiful house in Amityville, New York. The place seems perfect—spacious, picturesque, and a dream come true for any family looking to settle down. That's nearly exactly what happened to the Lutz family. But little did they know, their dream home would soon turn into a nightmare that would follow them for years to come.

But let's rewind a bit. Before the family moved in, something pretty grisly went down in that house. A year earlier, in 1974, a guy named Ronald DeFeo, Jr. went absolutely mad and murdered his entire family while they were sleeping. Creepy, right? Now, fast forward to when the Lutz family, George and Kathy, along with their three kids, moved in. They got a steal of a deal on the house—probably because, you know, it had a bit of a bad rap after the whole murder thing. But hey, who can resist a bargain, right?

Anyway, things started off okay-ish for the Lutzes, but it didn't take long for stuff to get really weird. They reported a plethora of crazy occurrences—doors slamming on their own, strange odors, cold spots, and even slime oozing out of the walls. And let's not forget the flies—swarms, even in the dead of winter. Not exactly your typical household pests.

But it didn't stop there. George claimed he saw red eyes peering at him from outside the house, and Kathy said she felt like she was being physically attacked by some unseen force. I mean, talk about a rough welcome to the neighborhood.

The Lutzes were so freaked out that they ended up bailing from the house after just twenty-eight days. Honestly, I can't blame them. But their story didn't end there. They spilled the tea to the world, and pretty soon, the Amityville Horror became a household name.

The Lutz family's story was the basis for the best-selling book and subsequent movie, *The Amityville Horror*, which depicted the family's harrowing experiences with the supernatural forces that seemed to inhabit the house. From those mysterious cold spots and foul odors to sightings of demonic entities and violent paranormal activity, the Lutz family's account of their time in the house has become among the most chilling and enduring ghost stories of all time.

And here's the kicker: The whole thing is still a hot debate. Some folks swear up and down the Lutzes were telling the truth, and the house really was haunted by some evil entity. Others say it was all a load of BS, just a publicity stunt to cash in on a tragedy. Who's right? Well, that's for you to decide.

But we do know one thing... The Amityville Horror House will go down in history as one of the spookiest tales of all time. And who knows? Maybe the dark entity is still out there, waiting for its next unsuspecting victims to move in and stir up some trouble.

The mystery surrounding the Amityville Horror House continues to intrigue those interested in true paranormal unsolved mysteries and psychic phenomena. The home remains a popular destination for paranormal enthusiasts and thrill-seekers looking to experience the unsettling atmosphere for themselves. Many visitors have reported feeling a sense of unease and dread while exploring the house, with some even claiming to have encountered ghostly apparitions and other mystifying occurrences.

Some believe the house is cursed or haunted by the restless spirits of its tragic past inhabitants, while others speculate there may be a more logical explanation for the strange things reported by the Lutz family and subsequent visitors to the home.

Whether you believe in ghosts or not, the tale of the Amityville Horror House is a compelling reminder of the unexplained mysteries that lie beyond our understanding, waiting to be explored and deciphered by those brave enough to venture into the unknown.

THE BELL WITCH HAUNTING

Here's another for lovers of true crime, paranormal occurrences, and unsolved mysteries. The story of the Bell Witch Haunting is a tale that continues to intrigue and baffle experts in the metaphysical field. It's among the most well-documented cases of supernatural activity in American history.

So, buckle up, because we're about to dive into one heck of a spooky story.

Imagine it's the early nineteenth century, in a little place called Adams, Tennessee. John Bell and his family are just minding their own business, living their lives like any other folks in rural America. But little did they know, they were about to become the stars of an infamous haunting in American history.

It all started innocently enough. Strange sounds, like scratching and knocking, echoing through the Bell household. At first, they brushed it off as the creaks and groans of an old house. But then things started getting seriously weird. The family claimed they heard disembodied voices whispering in the night, saw objects moving on their own, and even felt invisible hands slapping and pinching them. Yikes, right?

But here's where it gets really freaky. The Bells weren't the only ones experiencing this stuff. Word got out about the ghostly happenings, and soon enough, the whole community was talking about it. Even famous people like Andrew Jackson, who would later become the President of the United States, wanted to check out the commotion.

But it wasn't all fun and games. Things took a terrifying turn. The entity behind all the chaos—dubbed the Bell Witch—seemed to have a personal vendetta against John Bell and his family. It tormented them relentlessly, even going so far as to poison poor John, which ultimately led to his death in 1820. Now that's a serious grudge.

But the story doesn't end there. Even after John's death, the Bell Witch stuck around, continuing to haunt the family and wreak havoc on anyone who dared to cross its path. Despite efforts to rid the home of the entity—including exorcisms and prayer—the haunting persisted for several more years. It wasn't until a local preacher performed an exorcism in 1821 that the entity *finally* calmed down and disappeared—for the most part, anyway.

Now, whether you believe this story is up to you. Some folks say it's just a tall tale passed down through the generations, while others swear it's the real deal. But we know one thing.

The Bell Witch haunting has left an indelible mark on American folklore, and its legacy continues to send shivers down the spines of those who dare to hear its story. If you ever find yourself in Adams, Tennessee, keep an ear out for strange noises—you never know who—or what—you might encounter.

THE QUEEN MARY SHIP

The Queen Mary has long been a source of fascination. The majestic ocean liner, which sailed the seas from 1936 to 1967, is now permanently docked in Long Beach, California, where it serves as a floating hotel and museum. But beneath its elegant exterior lies a dark and mysterious history that continues to enthrall visitors and researchers alike.

So gather 'round, because we're about to set sail on a voyage through one of the spookiest ships to ever grace the seas—the RMS Queen Mary. She's not your average luxury liner. Oh, no, this ship has a haunted history that'll send shivers down your spine.

In the early 1930s, the Queen Mary was the epitome of luxury travel. From Hollywood stars to royalty, everyone who was anyone wanted a ticket to board the floating palace. But then World War II came along, and the Queen Mary traded in her plush accommodations for a stint as a troop transport ship. What a change of scenery.

The strange part? During her wartime service, the Queen Mary was involved in some pretty harrowing stuff. There were accidents, tragedies, and even a collision that resulted in the deaths of hundreds of sailors.

Despite being turned into a hotel and museum, the Queen Mary never quite shook off her haunted past. Guests and crew members alike report all sorts of ghostly encounters on board. From phantom footsteps echoing in empty corridors to apparitions appearing out of nowhere, the ship seems to have a life of its own—one that isn't always friendly.

One of the more famous ghostly residents is known as "The Lady in White." Legend has it she's the spirit of a young woman who tragically died on board and now wanders the ship in search of her lost love. Guests have reported seeing her walking the hallways or even dancing alone in the empty ballroom. Talk about a lonely afterlife.

But the Lady in White isn't the only guest aboard who's beyond the veil. One of the other most famous legends surrounding the Queen Mary is that of the "Gray Ghost," a nickname given to the ship during World War II when it was painted gray and used as a troopship. According to reports, the ship was haunted by the spirits of soldiers who died on board during the war. There are also tales of ghostly children playing in the swimming pool, a spectral sailor who roams the engine room, and even the ghost of a crew member who was crushed to death in one of the ship's doors. It's really and truly like a floating haunted house.

In addition to its paranormal activity, the Queen Mary is also home to a number of ancient mysteries. The ship's opulent Art Deco interior is filled with artifacts and relics from its heyday, including original furniture, artwork, and textures. Some visitors have reported feeling as though they have been transported back in time when walking through the ship's corridors, leading to speculation about the existence of time slips or portals.

Despite the many unanswered questions surrounding the Queen Mary, the iconic ship has grasped the imaginations of those who dare to explore its haunted halls. Whether you're a skeptic or a believer, the mysteries of the Queen Mary are sure to leave a lasting impression on anyone who dares to delve into its dark and enigmatic past. So, if you ever find yourself boarding this majestic ship, keep your eyes peeled and your wits about you.

THE TALLMAN FAMILY AND THE POSSESSED BUNK BED

Are you ready for another bone-chilling and fascinating tale? This is the haunting story of the Tallman family and their infamous bunk bed. It's a real-life horror that's guaranteed to send shivers down your spine.

Picture a scene straight out of *Stranger Things*. Back in the 1980s, in the small, quiet town of Horicon, Wisconsin, the Tallman family, consisting of Allen and Debbie and their three young children, moved into a seemingly ordinary home—a place they called their "dream home." Somewhere they hoped they could live and love forever. And everything appeared normal at first. Until they brought home a second-hand bunk bed for their kids...

Now, you'd think a bunk bed would just be a piece of furniture, right? Well, not this one. Shortly after bringing it home, the Tallman family's life turned into a living nightmare. The children started experiencing terrifying nightmares described as involving encounters with a dark and malevolent figure. In addition, while all three had previously been healthy kids, all were suddenly sick all the time.

One night, the son who was sleeping in the room next door to his sisters in the bunk bed, reported that his clock radio was changing channels, the dial going from one side to the other, increasingly fast. In the resulting static, voices could be heard.

All three kids would wake up screaming, claiming to have seen an ominous presence looming over their beds as they slept.

But it didn't stop there; not even while they were awake. Strange things began happening around the house. The Tallmans heard inexplicable noises like footsteps and whispers echoing through the halls at night. Not to mention the creepy shadows that seemed to lurk in the corners of their visions. And objects would move on their own—like the time Allen was painting, walked away, and came back to find the paintbrush moved and standing handle-down in the paint can feet away from where he'd rested it.

One night, as Allen returned home from his shift as a

manufacturing plant supervisor, he heard a strange voice calling to him. Urging him to "come here." He went around the house to investigate, hearing the beckoning whisper again, but didn't find anything. Suddenly, he saw his garage on fire. He raced inside, put his lunch pail down, and then ran back outside, only to see the garage no worse for wear. As he reentered the house and bent to pick up his lunchbox, it went flying across the room without him even touching it.

Not too long after, things took a more sinister turn. One night, Allen and Debbie heard their youngest screaming from her room. When they rushed in, they found her terrified and hysterical, claiming that a dark figure had tried to strangle her.

And then, one night when Alan was working a late shift, he asked one of his relatives to watch over the girls until they fell asleep. The family member was a complete skeptic and non-believer. However, as he lay on the floor of the girls' room, the same figure seen by the kids appeared to him. He screamed and ran from the room. Debbie heard him and asked what'd happened. He was visibly shaken, and that was the final straw. Debbie grabbed him and the kids and left.

Desperate for answers, the family reached out to paranormal experts and even local clergy for help. But no matter what they tried, the haunting only seemed to intensify. That's when they realized that the bunk bed was at the heart of all their strife.

Two weeks after the event with the family member, the Tallmans destroyed the bunk bed, moved to another city, and lived a seemingly normal life.

But the family's ordeal became a troubling tale, one that sent shockwaves through the community and captured the attention of paranormal enthusiasts worldwide. Even now, the Tallman family bunk bed haunting remains up there with the most perplexing cases of paranormal activity ever documented.

So, if you ever come across a second-hand bunk bed with a dark history, you might want to think twice before bringing it home. You never know what kind of nightmares it might unleash upon you.

THE MYRTLES PLANTATION

Step right up, because I'm about to take you on a spine-tingling journey through another of America's most haunted locations—the Myrtles Plantation. Get ready to meet the ghosts that still roam its halls and the frightening tales that have made this plantation a legendary hotspot for paranormal enthusiasts.

Nestled in St. Francisville, Louisiana, the Myrtles Plantation stands as a testament to the grandeur and tragedy of the Old South. With its stately columns, sweeping verandas, and sprawling grounds, it's the epitome of Southern charm. But beneath its picturesque façade lies a history steeped in mystery and ghostly lore.

The story begins in the early nineteenth century when the plantation was owned by General David Bradford. Legend has it the plantation's grounds are haunted by the spirits of those who suffered and died there, including slaves who toiled under brutal conditions, and other victims of violence and tragedy.

Chloe is our first ghostly resident, a slave woman said to have been involved in a tragic love affair with the plantation owner. According to folklore, after she was spurned, Chloe sought revenge by poisoning the family. Her ghost is said to wander the grounds, forever seeking redemption for her deeds.

But Chloe is just one of many spirits said to haunt the Myrtles. There's also the Woodruff children. Sarah and James Woodruff died of yellow fever in the nineteenth century and are said to haunt the plantation. Visitors have reported seeing the apparitions of children playing in the house and hearing their laughter echoing through the halls.

Then there's William Drew Winter, a former owner of the plantation. He is said to have been shot on the front porch of the house in the 1870s, and his ghost is rumored to haunt the property, with some accounts describing sightings of a man in nineteenth-century clothing wandering the grounds.

Visitors and staff alike have reported loads of bizarre phenomena, from mysterious footsteps and phantom touches to apparitions forming in mirrors and photographs. Some have even claimed to hear the sounds of ghostly voices and music drifting through the night.

Despite efforts to debunk the stories and explain away the phenomena, the Myrtles Plantation continuously draws in curious visitors and paranormal investigators from around the world. Its haunted reputation has earned it a spot on countless lists of the most haunted places in America and inspired books, movies, and TV shows exploring its ghostly lore.

So, if you're feeling brave, take a trip to the Myrtles Plantation and see for yourself. If you dare. But be warned, once you enter its hallowed halls, you may find yourself face-to-face with the spirits of the past, lingering on in the shadows of history.

PITTOCK MANSION

The Pittock Mansion, perched atop Portland's West Hills, is a stunning architectural marvel with a haunting history that adds an extra layer of intrigue to its grandeur. Let me spin you the tale of the Pittock Mansion haunting...

Built in 1914 as a dream home for Henry and Georgiana Pittock, the mansion boasts breathtaking views of the city and a luxurious interior adorned with opulent furnishings. But behind its elegant façade lies a story of heartbreak and mystery.

In 1918, tragedy struck the Pittock family when Georgiana passed away from diabetes. Henry, grief-stricken by the loss of his beloved wife, continued to reside in the mansion until his death in 1919. Following his passing, some believe the spirits of both Henry and Georgiana continued to linger within the mansion's walls.

Visitors and staff at the Pittock Mansion have reported numerous strange occurrences over the years. Strange noises, such as disembodied footsteps and whispers, have been heard echoing through the halls when no one else is around. Objects have been known to move on their own, and cold spots have been felt in certain areas of the house.

Those at the Pittock Mansion often encounter the apparition of a woman believed to be Georgiana Pittock. Witnesses have reported seeing her ghostly figure gliding through the rooms of the mansion, dressed in the attire of the early twentieth century.

Another eerie phenomenon associated with the mansion is the random appearance of phantom scents. Visitors have reported catching whiffs of perfume or cigar smoke without any logical explanation for their presence.

Despite the reports of ghostly activity, many visitors to the Pittock Mansion are drawn not only to its beauty but also to the rich history that permeates its halls. If you believe or if you don't, there's no denying the allure of the Pittock Mansion and the mystery that surrounds it. But at least these are friendly ghosts. Still, why are they there? Why do they make themselves known to people? And if nothing bad happened, why haunt the mansion at all?

THE WINCHESTER MYSTERY HOUSE

This story is one of my favorites. It's just so bizarre... Enough to make your head spin.

In the late nineteenth century, there was a wealthy widow named Sarah Winchester, heir to the massive fortune generated by the Winchester Repeating Arms Company.

But Sarah has a tragic backstory. Her husband and infant daughter both died, leaving her grief-stricken and alone. So, what's a grieving widow with a boatload of cash to do? Well, if you're Sarah Winchester, the answer is apparently to build a sprawling, labyrinthine mansion that defies all logic and reason.

Sarah bought a modest farmhouse in San Jose, California, and then proceeded to turn it into a mind-boggling maze of secret passages, dead ends, and staircases that led absolutely nowhere. Seriously, the place was like something straight out of a haunted house movie.

Legend has it Sarah was convinced she was cursed by the spirits of those killed by Winchester rifles. So, to appease the vengeful ghosts, she embarked on a never-ending construction project, adding room after room, staircase after staircase, until the mansion became a bewildering maze of confusion.

But it wasn't just the sheer size of the mansion that made it so strange. Sarah incorporated many odd features into the house, as well, like doors that opened onto blank walls, windows that overlooked other rooms, and staircases that led to the ceiling. There's even a room called the *Seance Room* where Sarah is said to have communed with spirits.

And get this. Construction on the Winchester Mystery House went on for nearly thirty-eight years, right up until Sarah's death in 1922. When all was said and done, the mansion boasted over one hundred and sixty rooms, including forty bedrooms, two ballrooms, and forty-seven fireplaces. And that's not even counting the secret passages and hidden chambers scattered throughout the house.

So, whether or not you believe the rumors about Sarah Winchester being haunted by vengeful spirits, we know the Winchester Mystery House is one heck of a weird and wacky place. If you ever find yourself in San Jose, do yourself a favor and take a tour. Just watch your step—you might end up lost in the maze of staircases and corridors, never to be seen again.

LEMP MANSION

The Lemp Mansion is a place so haunted, it'll make your hair stand on end.

In the late nineteenth century, in St. Louis, Missouri, the Lemp family was living the high life, running one of the top breweries in the country.

The Lemps were like the Rockefellers of the beer world, rolling in dough and living in luxury. They built a magnificent mansion in the grand Victorian style, complete with all the bells and whistles you'd expect from a family of their stature. But little did they know, their good fortune was about to take a dark and twisted turn.

Tragedy first struck the Lemp family in 1901 when Frederick Lemp, the heir to the brewery empire, died under mysterious circumstances. Some say it was suicide, others claim it was foul play, but regardless, his death cast a shadow over the family and the mansion.

But the grim reaper wasn't done with the Lemps yet. Over the years, the family was plagued by a string of misfortunes—bankruptcies, divorces, and untimely deaths that seemed to haunt them like a curse. Some say the mansion itself was cursed, a breeding ground for all manner of ghostly shenanigans.

But it gets weirder. The Lemp Mansion is said to be haunted by the restless spirits of the family members who met tragic ends within its walls. Guests and staff have reported a wide variety of scary phenomena—full-body apparitions appearing out of thin air, disembodied footsteps echoing through the halls, and objects moving on their own.

One of the most often seen haunts is said to be William Lemp, Jr., who tragically took his life in 1922. His ghost is rumored to linger in the mansion, sometimes appearing as a spectral figure or making his presence known with strange sounds and sensations.

But he's not the only one. The spirits of other Lemp family members, including Frederick's father, William Lemp, Sr., and his sister, Elsa, are said to haunt the mansion, as well. Some believe their restless souls are trapped within the manor's walls, doomed to wander for all eternity.

Believer or not, there's no denying the ominous atmosphere of the Lemp Mansion. It's become a hotspot for paranormal enthusiasts and thrill-seekers alike, all of them drawn to the mansion's dark history and haunted reputation. But if you're feeling brave, why not pay a visit?

THE MCPIKE MANSION

This one isn't quite as well known, but it's no less interesting.

This is the story of the McPike Mansion, a place with a haunted history that'll make your guts curl. In Alton,

Illinois, a wealthy businessman named Henry Guest McPike decided to build himself a grand mansion atop a hill overlooking the Mississippi River.

Now, McPike wasn't messing around when it came to his house. He spared no expense, decking it out with all the fancy trimmings of the nineteenth century—ornate architecture, sprawling gardens, the whole shebang. The McPike Mansion was the talk of the town, a symbol of the man's wealth and success.

But as the years went by, tragedy struck the McPike family. Henry McPike passed away, and the mansion fell into disrepair. Eventually, it was abandoned, left to decay and crumble into ruin. But that's when things started to get really interesting.

While the McPike Mansion was empty, it was far from uninhabited. Locals began to report strange happenings—mysterious lights flickering in the windows at night, indefinable noises echoing through the halls, and the unmistakable feeling of being watched by unseen eyes.

The mansion became a magnet for ghost hunters and paranormal enthusiasts, drawn to its haunted reputation like moths to a flame. And boy, did they find more than they bargained for. Some claimed to have seen ghostly apparitions wandering the grounds, while others reported feeling cold spots and sudden general drops in temperature.

But perhaps the most chilling encounter of all involves the spirit of a woman known as "Sarah." Legend has it Sarah was a servant who worked at the mansion and tragically lost her life there. Her ghost is said to roam the grounds, sometimes appearing as a misty figure or making her presence known with strange noises and disembodied voices.

There's also Henry's mother, Lydia. She was the matriarch of the family and is a very strong presence, even in death. McPike's wife, Mary, also makes regular appearances. She's said to be shy but to love children.

No earthly bodies have lived in the house since 1954 —it was long ago condemned—but the site is still a hotbed of activity.

FRANKLIN CASTLE

This one is equal parts spooky and intriguing—the story of Franklin Castle, a place with a history so haunted, it'll give you goose bumps.

We're in Cleveland, Ohio for this one, and a wealthy banker named Hannes Tiedemann decides to build himself a grand mansion that'll make all the neighbors jealous.

Tiedemann goes all out, constructing a massive stone fortress that's straight out of a gothic novel. Towers, turrets, gargoyles—the whole nine yards. Franklin Castle was like something out of a fairy tale—more like the Grimm brothers wrote—but little did anyone know, it would soon become the stuff of nightmares.

You see, despite its grand appearance, Franklin Castle had a dark and twisted history lurking within its walls. Rumors swirled about secret passages, hidden rooms, and even a mysterious series of deaths that seemed to plague the Tiedemann family.

Legend has it that tragedy struck the Tiedemanns

soon after they moved into the mansion. Several of their children passed away under mysterious circumstances, leading some to suspect foul play. But others claimed the deaths were the result of a family curse, passed down from generation to generation.

The spooky happenings were—and are—vast and varied. Visitors to Franklin Castle report all sorts of eerie phenomena—strange noises in the night, ghostly shadow figures wandering the halls, and even encounters with the spirits of those who had met untimely ends within its walls.

The most often-seen ghostly resident of Franklin Castle is said to be a woman in black, believed to be the ghost of Tiedemann's niece, who tragically died in the mansion. Witnesses have reported seeing her apparition wandering the grounds, sometimes accompanied by the sound of sobbing or the rustle of her mourning attire.

Outside of the ghosts, the mansion's secret passages and hidden rooms themselves add to the air of mystery and intrigue. Some say they were used by Tiedemann for nefarious purposes, while others claim they were simply a product of his eccentricity. We may never know the truth.

THE BOISE MURDER HOUSE

Let's talk about the infamous Boise Murder House and its supposed hauntings. This place has quite a reputation, so grab a seat and get ready for a spooky story.

Back in the 1980s, the house on Linden Street gained infamy due to a gruesome murder that took place there.

Now, with its soot-covered walls, broken windows, and haphazard boards, it looks like something from a horror-movie set. But the truth could be even scarier.

This two-story Craftsman, known also as the "Chop-Chop House," is the site of an absolutely grisly killing. In the early morning hours of June 30th, 1987, thirty-seven-year-old Daniel Rodgers and thirty-one-year-old Daron Cox shot and killed twenty-one-year-old Preston Murr in the basement of Rodgers's home at 805 W Linden Street. The two men then used an ax and knife to dismember the corpse, wrapped the pieces in plastic bags, and drove to the Idaho-Oregon border to dump the body parts in the Brownlee Reservoir. Horrifying as the facts of the crime are, there is one detail more haunting than the rest. Murr almost escaped.

A neighbor called the police during the argument and attack, but they never responded. The next morning, the guy called again to report blood on his screen door, and they finally showed up. The blood found throughout the neighborhood—on sidewalks and at least one other house—painted a macabre and harrowing picture of Murr's desperate attempt to escape his murderers the night before.

While the crime scene has long since been cleaned up, a dark miasma still surrounds the house.

People claim to have experienced a multitude of bizarre happenings inside the Linden Street house. From strange noises echoing through the halls to flickering lights and objects mysteriously moving on their own, it's the stuff horror movies are made of. Some even say they've seen creeping, crawling shadow figures entering and exiting the rooms, trapped in a never-ending cycle of anguish. And the basement has always felt *off* to people.

One tale goes that one of the subsequent owners and his friend thought they heard someone trying to break into the house. When they went out to the front porch to look, no one was there. After searching the front yard, the owner turned to face the house and saw what he called a "big, black, oily-looking thing" in the upstairs window. He remembers seeing the shadow-y figure move away from the window and to the bedroom door before it disappeared. Shortly after, it reappeared outside in a mirror sitting on the porch. He watched as the black ball moved down the large column, slowly getting bigger until it took up the entire reflection of the mirror and moved right through him. "It was the weirdest, most disturbing thing I've ever felt and just typing this makes me feel it again. It's like ice fingers sinking into my shoulders," he said.

Despite this—and many other—anecdotes, several people insist the house isn't haunted. The family who lived there in 2008 and 2009 said they never had any strange happenings. Skeptic or believer, there's no denying the charged atmosphere that surrounds this place. Locals often avoid it like the plague, fearing what might lurk within its shadowy confines. And while some thrill-seekers dare to venture inside in search of a paranormal encounter, many leave with their nerves frayed and their imaginations running wild.

But hey, who knows what really goes on behind closed doors? Maybe the Boise Murder House is just a spooky old building with a sinister past, or perhaps there's something more evil lurking within its walls. Whatever the truth may be, one thing's for sure—it's not a place for the faint of heart.

THE OLD LOUISVILLE MURDER HOUSE

This story is gruesome, grisly, and sad—especially given the hatred that lies beneath its history. If you want the complete story, I highly recommend David Domine's book *A Dark Room in Glitter Ball City: Murder, Secrets, and Scandals in Old Louisville*. But let me give you a rundown...

The home at 1435 S. 4th St is an eight-thousand-square-foot abode built in 1897. At one time in the 1900s, it served as an osteopathic practice and sanitorium —with some *very* questionable practices. And if that wasn't bad enough, it became the site of a horrible crime in 2010.

Jeffrey Mundt, a top official at Northwestern University, nursed an unhealthy appetite for rough sex and crystal meth. In 2007, Mundt moved to Louisville, Kentucky and bought a house on well-known 4th Street.

In 2009, Jeffrey met Joey Banis on an internet dating site, and after only a few weeks of being together, Joey moved into the Old Louisville mansion.

Fast forward a year later, to the fateful night of June 17, 2010, where 911 gets a call from Mundt, telling them Banis was attempting to attack him with a hammer after Jeff tried to break up with him.

When the police arrived and confronted Banis about the assault, he gave them more than they ever imagined.

He suddenly blurted out that his boyfriend had murdered someone in 2009 and revealed that the victim's name was Jamie Carroll.

He told the police that right before the murder, Mundt had recently lost his job and needed money to keep up his lifestyle, so he invited Jamie Carroll—a known drug dealer—over for drugs. Yes, he wanted the meth, but he also wanted to rob the poor guy blind.

Banis went on to say that they were all high, and Mundt was in bed with Carroll when things went sideways. Jeff began attacking Jamie, stabbing him over and over. Joey then said Jeff pulled out a gun and shot Carroll and then threatened Joey to help him dispose of the corpse. They dragged the body downstairs and buried him in the dirt floor of the basement.

Unsure whether or not to believe Joey, the police decided to investigate. They searched the basement and found a buried Rubbermaid tub with the remains of Jamie Carroll inside. They also found blood in the bathtub and signs of a bullet hole in the wall, corroborating Joey Banis's story.

Jeff pointed the finger at Joey, of course, citing his continued violent behavior.

What was the motive for this heinous crime? Jealousy. Joey and Jamie were lovers and Jeffrey didn't like it. He didn't like Jamie much at all.

The two went to trial. Banis was given twenty years to life, but because of a video found on his computer, Mundt was found not guilty of murder and only charged with tampering. He was sentenced to eight years but only served one, getting out on parole in 2014.

In the years following the crime, the home has been several private residences and even off-campus housing. And through it all, it has been said to constantly feel oppressive and be a hotbed of paranormal activity. It's been featured on countless TV shows, including *Hell House* on Investigation Discovery.

And while it has *loads* of similarities to the house depicted on *American Horror Story*, the timing is off, and those things are just coincidence. Or are they? Perhaps there are some other paranormal things at work.

Chapter Two

Mysterious Disappearances and Unexplained Phenomena

In the realm of the unknown, few stories grip the imagination quite like those of mysterious disappearances. From vanishing without a trace in the wilderness to inexplicable disappearances from crowded urban centers or the open sea, these cases defy logical explanation and leave investigators shaking their heads in bewilderment.

Here, we dive into the perplexing world of vanished souls and the circumstances surrounding their disappearances. From the enigmatic case of the Mary Celeste, a ghost ship found adrift with no crew aboard, to the supernatural tale of the Lost Colony of Roanoke, where an entire settlement vanished without leaving a single clue behind, the mysteries explored here will leave you questioning the very fabric of reality.

Join me as we make our way into the heart of the unknown, where the boundaries between fact and fiction blur, and the answers remain tantalizingly out of reach. These are the tales of those who vanished into thin air, leaving behind nothing but questions and speculation. Welcome to the enigmatic world of mysterious disappearances and unexplained phenomena.

THE BERMUDA TRIANGLE

Roughly bounded by Miami, Bermuda, and Puerto Rico, the Bermuda Triangle is a region in the western part of the North Atlantic Ocean where a number of aircraft and ships are said to have disappeared under mysterious circumstances.

So, what's the deal with this so-called "Devil's Triangle?" Well, it all started gaining notoriety back in the mid-twentieth century when reports began surfacing about ships and aircraft disappearing without a trace in the area. Now, we're not talking about just a couple of incidents here. We're talking about a string of disappearances that seemed to defy all logic and explanation.

One of the best cases is that of Flight 19, a squadron of U.S. Navy bombers that vanished during a training mission in 1945. Despite dedicated search efforts, neither the planes nor the crew were ever found. And when they sent the rescue planes out to search for them, they *also* mysteriously disappeared.

But wait, there's more! Ships have also met their doom in the Bermuda Triangle. Take the case of the U.S.S. Cyclops, a massive Navy cargo ship that vanished without a trace in 1918, along with its three hundred crew members. To date, no wreckage has ever been found, leaving experts scratching their heads in disbelief.

Now, before you start canceling your vacation plans

to Bermuda, it's worth noting that the Bermuda Triangle isn't necessarily the Bermuda Square of doom and despair. Sure, it's had its fair share of strange happenings, but plenty of ships and planes sail through or fly over the area without any issues.

Scientists and skeptics have proposed various theories to explain the mysteries of the Bermuda Triangle, ranging from magnetic anomalies messing with navigation equipment to freak weather phenomena and good old-fashioned human error. And while these explanations might debunk some of the more outlandish theories (sorry, aliens and sea monsters), they don't quite satisfy everyone.

So, the Bermuda Triangle holds true as one of the world's greatest unsolved mysteries, a place where fact and legend blur together in a swirling vortex of intrigue. A tantalizing enigma that defies rational explanation. Regardless of where you fall on the belief scale, you can bank on one thing —the Bermuda Triangle will likely continue to capture our imaginations for years to come, and the stories and legends surrounding the mysterious region will keep intriguing and mystifying those with a thirst for the unknown.

THE SUPERSTITION MOUNTAINS

All right, my friends, let me spin you a tale as old as the dust-covered peaks themselves—the legend of the Superstition Mountains. Nestled in the rugged terrain of Arizona, these ancient mountains have long been shrouded in mystery and intrigue, earning a reputation as being among the most enigmatic places in the American West.

Legend has it that deep within the labyrinthine canyons and rocky crags of the Superstitions lies the Lost Dutchman's Mine, a fabled trove of gold so vast and rich that it has driven countless fortune seekers to madness in their quest to find it. But the Superstition Mountains are not just home to stories of lost treasure—they're also steeped in tales of supernatural phenomena and eerie encounters that defy the rational mind.

Many who have ventured into the depths of the Superstitions have reported strange sights and sounds, from ghostly apparitions drifting through the mist-shrouded valleys to inexplicable lights dancing on the horizon. Some claim to have heard disembodied voices whispering in the wind, while others speak of a palpable sense of unease that settles over them like a heavy cloak as they explore the rugged terrain.

And then there's the Apache Death Cave, a cavern said to be cursed by the spirits of the Indigenous Peoples who met their end within its dark depths. According to legend, those who dare to enter the cave are doomed to suffer a fate worse than death itself, haunted by vengeful spirits that lurk in the shadows, waiting to claim their souls.

Despite the dangers and mysteries that abound in the Superstition Mountains, brave adventurers continue to flock to their rugged slopes in search of answers and adventure. Some seek the elusive treasure of the Lost Dutchman's Mine, while others are drawn by the allure of the unknown, eager to uncover the secrets that lie hidden beneath the rocky soil.

The Superstition Mountains will always hold a special place in the annals of American folklore, a place where fact and fiction blur together in a swirling maelstrom of mystery and wonder. So, if you ever find yourself wandering the dusty trails of Arizona, keep one eye on the horizon and one hand on your heart, for you never know what secrets the Superstitions may hold.

THE ROANOKE COLONY

If you've read my other nonfiction book, *The Dark Side of Humanity: True Crime Stories To Curl Up With,* you've read a bit about the next two entries in this chapter. But they fit so well in here, I had to tell them again for those who are just picking this up.

The year is 1587, and a group of English settlers led by a man named John White, set sail for the New World, eager to establish a permanent colony in the land we now know as North Carolina. They arrive at Roanoke Island, a lush and promising land teeming with potential.

Now, things start off pretty well for the settlers. They build homes, plant crops, and forge relationships with the local Indigenous tribes. But trouble soon brews on the horizon. Supplies run low, tensions rise, and before long, John White is forced to return to England for reinforcements and provisions, leaving his wife, daughter, and granddaughter behind.

And then things took a bizarre turn. When White finally returns to Roanoke three years later, he finds the settlement deserted, with no sign of his family or any of the other colonists. The only thing left behind is a word carved into a wooden post, and the letters C, R, and O etched into a nearby tree. The word? *CROATOAN*.

Theories have abounded regarding what happened to the inhabitants of Roanoake, from alien abductions to cannibalism to, as the hit TV show *Supernatural* posited in the season two episode, a demonic virus. But the truth is far less sensational.

The name "Croatoan" referred to an Indigenous tribe that was friendly with the settlers who lived on nearby Hatteras Island. Broken down, ethnologists and anthropologists believe the word may have been a combination of two Algonquian words meaning "talk town" or "council town," and could be a clue as to where the so-called lost colony went. But strangely, no one looked on the nearby island and simply assumed all the residents had been murdered or worse.

So, what happened to the lost colony of Roanoke? Well, that's the million-dollar question, my friends, and it's one that has baffled historians and sparked endless speculation for centuries.

Whatever the truth may be, the mystery of the lost colony of Roanoke will likely capture the imagination and spark debate for generations to come. Perhaps one day, we'll uncover the truth behind one of America's greatest unsolved mysteries. But until then, the story of Roanoke remains a haunting reminder of the enigmatic and sometimes obscure nature of our past.

. . .

THE DYATLOV PASS INCIDENT

Another weird one, dear readers. One that fits both the unsolved mysteries and the paranormal phenomena categories.

Strap in, because I'm about to tell you about one of the best and most bizarre mysteries to ever grip the icy heart of the Russian wilderness—the Dyatlov Pass Incident.

It all started in 1959, when a group of nine experienced hikers set out on an expedition to the Ural Mountains in Soviet Russia. Led by the intrepid Igor Dyatlov, these adventurers were determined to conquer the unforgiving peaks and valleys of the northern wilderness.

When the group failed to check in as planned, search parties were dispatched to find them. What they discovered sent shivers down their spines.

The hikers' campsite was in absolute shambles, with tents torn open from the inside as if the occupants had fled in a blind panic. The reason was unknown. Footprints led away from the campsite, some barefoot, as if the hikers had fled into the freezing cold without proper clothing, but none seemed to return.

As searchers combed the area, they made a series of grisly discoveries. The bodies of the hikers were found scattered across the snowy landscape, some partially clothed and with signs of trauma that defied explanation. One victim had a fractured skull, another had their tongue inexplicably ripped out.

And the weirdest part? Despite exhaustive investigations by Soviet authorities, no satisfactory explanation was *ever* found for what happened to the hikers that fateful night. Some speculated that an avalanche swept through the camp, while others whispered of yetis or hostile encounters with local tribes.

There's also a theory that something otherworldly was at play—a notion fueled by reports of strange lights in the sky and other unexplainable things in the area around the time of the incident.

To this day, the Dyatlov Pass Incident is still at the top of the list as one of the more baffling and haunting mysteries in the annals of paranormal lore. What really happened on that remote mountainside? The truth may be lost to time, forever shrouded in the icy depths of the Russian wilderness.

PERCY HARRISON FAWCETT

In 1925, the military man and courageous explorer Percy Harrison Fawcett sets out on a quest to uncover the lost city of "Z" in the heart of the Amazon rainforest. With him are his son, Jack, and Jack's best friend, Raleigh Rimell. Their mission? To find evidence of a fabled ancient civilization hidden deep within the jungle.

Now, Fawcett was no stranger to adventure. He'd already made several expeditions into the Amazon, braving disease, hostile tribes, and the unforgiving terrain in search of his elusive goal. But this time, something was different. Something was...off.

As the days stretched into weeks and the weeks into months, Fawcett's communications grew increasingly sporadic. Then, one day, they stopped altogether. No letters, no updates—nothing. It was as if the jungle had swallowed them whole.

Despite numerous rescue missions and search efforts, Fawcett, his son, and Rimell were never seen or heard from again. They vanished without a trace, with only rumors and speculation remaining.

Over the years, countless theories have emerged to explain their disappearance. Some say they fell victim to disease or starvation, while others speculate that they were captured by hostile tribes or succumbed to the perils of the jungle.

Another theory is that Fawcett and his companions stumbled upon something...otherworldly—a lost civilization, perhaps? Or a portal to another dimension hidden deep within the Amazon?

The disappearance of Percy Harrison Fawcett persists as one of the greatest unsolved mysteries in the annals of exploration. What happened to him and his companions? Did they meet a tragic end at the hands of the jungle, or did they uncover secrets that were never meant to be discovered? The truth may never be known.

THE DISAPPEARANCE OF THE AUSTRALIAN PRIME MINISTER

Okay, let's dive into a tale that's utterly baffling. The haunting disappearance of Australian Prime Minister Harold Holt.

In December 17, 1967, Holt was taking a leisurely swim at Cheviot Beach near Melbourne. Now, you'd think the Prime Minister would have a whole entourage of security guards and aides with him, but nope, Holt was known for his love of the ocean and often went swimming alone.

So, there he is, enjoying a sunny day at the beach, when he suddenly vanishes without a trace. Poof, gone, like a ghost in the waves. And despite extensive search efforts involving helicopters, divers, and even the Royal Australian Navy, no sign of Holt was ever found.

Now you might be thinking, *"Okay, maybe he drowned or got swept away by a rip current."* Could be. But Cheviot Beach was known for its calm waters, and Holt was an experienced swimmer. Plus, there were no strong currents or storms reported that day. It's as if he simply...vanished into thin air.

Of course, with such a high-profile figure disappearing under such mysterious circumstances, conspiracy theories abound. Some say Holt faked his own death and went into hiding, while others hypothesize that he was abducted by foreign agents or even taken by aliens.

Perhaps Holt met his end at the hands of something...supernatural. Some locals believe that Cheviot Beach is haunted by the spirits of sailors who perished in shipwrecks off the coast, and that Holt fell victim to their restless souls.

The disappearance of Harold Holt remains one of Australia's greatest unsolved mysteries. What really happened to the Prime Minister that fateful day? Was it foul play, or did he simply slip into the shadows? We may never know. What we do know is that Holt's disappearance continues to haunt the collective imagination of Australians and paranormal enthusiasts alike.

. . .

AMELIA EARHART

Care to take a flight with me into one of the greatest enduring mysteries of the twentieth century? Let's discuss the haunting tale of Amelia Earhart.

Amelia Earhart was no ordinary woman. She was a fearless aviator, a trailblazer who dared to defy the odds and take to the skies at a time when few women dared to dream of such adventures.

But on July 2, 1937, Earhart and her navigator, Fred Noonan, embarked on what would become their final flight—a daring attempt to circumnavigate the globe. Their plane, the Lockheed Electra, vanished somewhere over the vast expanse of the Pacific Ocean, leaving only questions and supposition that would haunt the world for decades to come.

Despite a wide net cast by the U.S. Navy and Coast Guard, no sign of Earhart, Noonan, or their plane was ever found. It was as if they had simply *poofed*, only a faint echo of their final radio transmissions remaining.

They must have simply crashed into the ocean, right? Maybe, but things are a little more mysterious. Some reports suggest distress calls were received from Earhart's plane days after it disappeared, leading to speculation that they may have crash-landed on a remote island and survived for a time before perishing.

Another tantalizing belief is that Earhart and Noonan didn't simply crash—they were abducted by extraterrestrial beings. Some conspiracy theorists believe that Earhart's plane was intercepted by a UFO and whisked away to another dimension or planet with no trace of their existence.

To this day, the disappearance of Amelia Earhart defies explanation and leaves a mark on aviation history. What really happened to this daring aviatrix and her navigator on that fateful day? Did they die tragically, or did they end up on a surprise journey into the unknown, bequeathing a legacy of courage and curiosity that endures and inspires us to this day? No matter what happened, Earhart's spirit of adventure will forever soar among the clouds, a beacon of hope and wonder in a world full of mysteries.

ANGELA HAMMOND

Back in 1991, on a quiet night in Clinton, Missouri, Angela Hammond, a young woman with a heart full of dreams and a spirit as free as the wind, was chatting on a payphone with her fiancé, Rob Shafer. Suddenly, Angela's words turned to screams.

Rob, who was on the other end of the line, immediately sprang into action, racing to Angela's aid. But by the time he arrived at the payphone, all he saw were the taillights of a green pickup. Shafer slammed his car into reverse gear to give chase, but blew its transmission in the process, helplessly watching as the abductor and Angela vanished into the night like ghosts in the wind.

Despite extensive search efforts by law enforcement and the community, Angela was never found. It was as if she had been swallowed whole by the darkness, leaving nothing but confusion and anguish for her loved ones. It could be linked to two other Missouri disappearances earlier that year, but detectives categorized the case as a random crime since Angela wasn't doing anything wrong or suspicious. Her abductor just happened to spot her talking to her boyfriend.

But this is weird. Months after Angela's disappearance, a local resident reported a disturbing sight—a green pickup truck submerged in a nearby river. Could this be the same vehicle Angela had described on that fateful night? Could it hold the key to unlocking the mystery of her disappearance?

Unfortunately, it yielded no answers, and Angela's fate remains unknown to this day. Some believe she was abducted by a serial killer who roamed the area, preying on young women. Others mention supernatural forces being at play, suggesting that Angela's spirit still wanders the dark streets of Clinton, searching for justice and closure.

All these years later, the disappearance of Angela Hammond still haunts the small Missouri town and the hearts of those who loved her. What really happened to this vibrant young woman on that fateful night? Why were the police not able to find the conspicuous green truck with a big decal on the window? Did she fall victim to a human predator, or did she encounter something...otherworldly? We may never know.

JAMES EDWARD TEDFORD

Back in the early 1940s, following the end of World War II, fifty-six-year-old James Edward Tedford was just an ordinary man living in a bustling Vermont town with his twenty-eight-year-old wife, Pearl. He worked as a handyman at a local hotel and led a quiet, unassuming life. Until he returned home one day to find his wife missing. He had no idea where she had gone. The last anyone had seen of her, she was walking to an Amoco store.

In 1947, James checked himself into a soldier's home, defeated and lonely.

But one fateful night two years later in December of 1949, Tedford boarded a bus bound for Bennington, Vermont, and also disappeared without a trace.

Now, you might be thinking, *"What's so mysterious about a guy taking a bus?"* Well, here's where things get strange. According to fourteen witnesses, they remember seeing Tedford board the bus, take a seat near the front, and go to sleep. But when the bus arrived in Bennington, he was nowhere to be found—nobody saw the man getting off the bus at any point in his journey.

What makes this case even stranger is that Tedford's belongings were still on the bus—his coat, his luggage, even an open bus timetable. It was as if he had simply vanished into thin air during the trip, with no clues or explanations for his disappearance.

Some speculate that Tedford may have gotten off the bus at a rest stop and met with foul play, while others talk of supernatural forces, suggesting he may have been abducted by aliens or spirited away to another dimension.

Maybe Tedford fell victim to the curse of Glastenbury Mountain—a remote and atmospheric wilderness area near Bennington that's known for its strange disappearances and unexplainable happenings.

The disappearance of James Edward Tedford remains like a black hole of the unknown. What really happened to this ordinary man on that cold December night? Did he encounter something that defies explanation? Tedford's disappearance still consumes the mind and haunts those who dare to ponder its enigmatic depths.

FRIEDER LANGER

This is another story of the so-called Bennington Triangle, a term coined by storyteller and broadcaster Joseph A. Citro. Citro is a well-known figure when it comes to the folklore, legends, and ghost stories of New England, but particularly Vermont. While conducting local research, he uncovered a number of disappearances in the area—including Telford's—and, with a touch of urban legend and folklore, came up with the now-infamous Bennington Triangle theory.

The Bennington Triangle soon became synonymous with strange occurrences, unsolved mysteries, and strange tales, largely thanks to Citro's dedication to documentation.

The *triangle* is set around Glastenbury Mountain and encompasses the surrounding ghost towns of Glastenbury and Somerset, as well as Bennington, Woodford, and Shaftsbury.

While the area has seen its fair share of weird events and disappearances, five that took place between 1945 and 1950 stand out.

One of those is the disappearance of Mrs. Frieder Langer.

Fifty-three-year-old Frieder Langer went camping with her cousin Herbert Elsner and at least one other family member on October 28, 1950 when she disappeared. The family had set up a campsite near Somerset Reservoir, and Langer and Elsner left the campsite to go on a hike on the nearby mountain. During their trip, Langer slipped into a stream. She requested that her cousin wait as she rushed back to the campsite to change her wet clothes. But she never returned.

Herbert headed back and discovered that his cousin had *not* gone back to the campsite. A two-week search effort ensued, with a helicopter and an aircraft as part of the search operation, but they couldn't find any trace of her. A year later, Langer's body mysteriously appeared near the same reservoir the searchers had extensively combed. Due to the conditions of her remains, it became difficult to determine the cause of her death—Langer was the last person to disappear in the triangle and the only one whose body was ever found.

For more than two centuries, there have been numerous sightings of a Bigfoot-like creature that locals began calling the "Bennington Monster." One of the first reported incidents was in the early 1800s when a stagecoach was forced to stop on a washed-out road. The driver noticed some huge footprints in the mud, much too large to be human. Then the coach was attacked by a giant creature who knocked the vehicle on its side, allowing the frightened passengers to only see a pair of eyes before the monster roared and disappeared into the trees. But in addition to the Bigfoot sightings and disappearances, others have reported seeing strange floating lights, other mysterious woodland creatures, and UFO activity.

Though no direct connections have been found that tie the Bennington Triangle cases together, other than geographic area and time period, some claim the disappearances were the work of a serial killer. Others blame an Indigenous curse or the paranormal, stating the place is a window into the unexplained. Some say the area is unstable due to wind patterns that are unusually chaotic and confusing, so people can easily get lost.

Whatever the reason, the area is famous for its strange phenomena.

THE SODDER CHILDREN

A tale as heart-wrenching as it is mysterious, the history of the Sodder children will captivate for many years to come.

It all started on Christmas Eve 1945 in Fayetteville, West Virginia. George and Jennie Sodder, along with their nine children—one older son was away in the military—were basking in a day of festive celebrations. When the parents told the kids it was time for bed, five of them asked if they could stay up and play with their new toys. The parents agreed, and they and the other children went on upstairs.

Then a strange series of events began.

The phone rang, and when the kids' mother answered, the voice on the other end asked for someone

42

unknown to her. When she said she didn't know the person in question, the voice on the other end laughed and immediately hung up. As she headed back to bed, Jennie noticed that someone had raised all the shades and unlocked all the doors. And the lights were on.

She and her husband later woke to a sound on the roof, only to realize the house was on fire. George and Jennie managed to escape along with four of their children, but the five who had stayed up—Maurice, Martha, Louis, Jennie, and Betty—were nowhere to be found and thus trapped inside.

Now, you'd think that would likely be the end of the tragic story, but things get even more mysterious. Despite harrowing and exhausting search efforts, no trace of the missing children was ever found. No bodies, no bones, nothing. It was as if they had simply vanished amid the chaos of the fire.

But that's not all. As investigators combed through the rubble of the Sodder home, they made a series of baffling discoveries. As mentioned, there were no human remains found in the ashes, and some witnesses claimed to have seen the children *after* the fire had started.

As the years passed, the Sodder family refused to give up hope, launching their own investigation into the mysterious disappearance of their children. They hired private detectives, conducted interviews, and erected a billboard near their home with pictures of the missing kids, pleading for information. They never stopped believing their children were still alive, even when the *official* conclusion was that they had succumbed to the inferno. Their sliver of hope was backed by a photo of one of their sons as a grown adult, mailed anonymously in the 1960s.

But despite their efforts, the fate of the Sodder children holds steady as one of the greatest unsolved mysteries in American history. Some believe they actually did perish in the fire, the remains somehow completely reduced to ash, while others think maybe they were kidnapped or taken by someone with malicious intent.

Did they survive? Were they taken? What do you think?

THE SARAH JOE

This tale begins in February 1979 on the tranquil island of Maui, Hawaii. A group of five friends set out on a fishing expedition aboard a small boat named the Sarah Joe. They were a tight-knit crew, adventurous souls who loved nothing more than exploring the pristine waters of the Pacific Ocean.

But on this fateful day, tragedy struck. A sudden storm swept across the area, catching the Sarah Joe and its crew off guard. As the winds howled and the waves crashed against the boat, the crew found themselves fighting for their lives in a desperate battle against the elements.

Despite their best efforts, the Sarah Joe and its crew were never seen again. Weeks turned into months, and months turned into years, but there was no sign of the missing boat or its occupants.

Then, in 1988, nearly a decade after the Sarah Joe

disappeared, a remarkable discovery was made. The wreckage of the boat was found on a remote atoll in the Marshall Islands—thousands of miles away from where it had last been seen.

But there's more. Alongside the wreckage were the skeletal remains of one of the crew members, Scott Moorman. It was as if the Sarah Joe had been transported to another realm, a ghostly echo of its former self. As they examined the grave and body closer, they saw something else. Several blank pieces of paper, about three inches square, with what looked to be tinfoil between the pages were stacked on the man's chest. They couldn't determine what it might be, and finally determined that further exploration of the gravesite would be disrespectful.

Despite additional research, the fate of the other crew members remains unknown. Some believe they perished at sea, while others whisper of supernatural forces at play during their ill-fated journey. And nobody knows who built the cairn to the deceased crew member. It almost appeared to be an ancient Chinese burial tradition, where small pieces of paper with gold or silver foil were placed in the coffin to be used as provisions in the afterlife.

But there's another far-out option. Maybe the Sarah Joe was caught in a time loop—a vortex of energy that transported the boat and its crew to another time or dimension. What's your take?

Chapter Three

Psychic Powers and Unsolved Crimes

HERE'S where the lines between the ordinary and the extraordinary blur into a interesting mix of mystery and intrigue. This chapter digs a bit more into the realm of the paranormal, exploring the remarkable abilities of individuals who claim to possess psychic gifts, and their uncanny connections to some of history's most baffling unsolved mysteries. From psychics who claim to communicate with the spirits of the deceased to those who profess to have visions of past events, the things that have played out in history will have you questioning the limits of human perception and the tantalizing possibilities of the unknown. Let's unravel the enigmatic threads that bind psychic powers and unsolved crimes, delving into the depths of the supernatural in search of answers that lie just beyond the reach of ordinary investigation.

PSYCHIC DETECTIVES

Let me take you on a trip into the intriguing world of

the psychic detective—a realm where the supernatural meets the sleuthing of unsolved mysteries.

These individuals claim to possess extraordinary abilities that allow them to assist law enforcement agencies in solving crimes. From communicating with spirits to receiving visions of past events, they offer a unique perspective on investigations that often defy conventional methods.

Now, you may be asking, "*Who are some of the most known psychic detectives?*"

Well, let me tell you.

Known for her alleged psychic abilities and claims of reincarnation, Dorothy Allison has captivated lovers of true crime and the supernatural for decades.

Dorothy Allison was born in 1924 in New Jersey, and from a young age, she exhibited extraordinary psychic abilities. She claimed to have visions and premonitions that seemed to defy rational explanation, leaving those around her both fascinated and unnerved.

But it wasn't until the 1950s that Dorothy's psychic powers would thrust her into the spotlight of the paranormal world. In 1953, Dorothy became involved in perhaps the most baffling unsolved mystery of the time—the disappearance of a young boy named Jimmy Sullivan.

Jimmy had vanished without a trace from his home in New Jersey, leaving behind a distraught family and a community desperate for answers. Enter Dorothy Allison, who claimed to have a vision of Jimmy's fate—a vision that led her to a remote wooded area where she believed Jimmy's body could be found.

Against all odds, Dorothy's vision proved to be eerily

accurate. Jimmy's remains were discovered exactly where she had described, sending shockwaves through the community and sparking speculation about the true nature of Dorothy's psychic abilities.

But Dorothy's work didn't end there. Over the years, she continued to assist law enforcement agencies in their investigations, using her psychic gifts to shed light on unsolved crimes and missing persons cases.

Despite skepticism from some quarters, Dorothy Allison remained steadfast in her belief that her psychic abilities were a force for good, helping to bring closure to grieving families and uncovering truths that had eluded conventional methods of investigation.

The story of Dorothy Allison and her extraordinary psychic powers continues to fascinate and mystify, and there's no denying the impact that Dorothy's visions had on the world around her, shining a light into the shadows of the unknown and offering hope in the face of uncertainty.

Besides Dorothy, one of the most prolific psychic detectives of all time is Noreen Renier. Renier rose in popularity in the 1970s and 1980s for her work on high-profile cases, including murders, kidnappings, and missing persons events. She claimed to receive information about the cases through visions and impressions, providing law enforcement with valuable leads that sometimes led to breakthroughs in the investigations.

Renier's specialty is psychometry—holding on to an item belonging to a missing or exploited person, from which she derives the ability to *become* that person. As she explains, "There will be times I will be Noreen, so if you really want Kimberly to see something, you have to say, 'Now Kimberly, we want you to tell us.'... It'll be a mixture, and I'll probably have the bad guy in there too occasionally."

One of the high-profile cases Renier worked on was the murder of Laci Peterson, who went missing in Modesto, California, in 2002. Laci's mother-in-law contacted Renier and asked her for help. Noreen used one of Laci's shoes, sent to her by Laci's husband Scott Peterson—who was subsequently convicted of the murder. Renier later said that she does not know whether police used her information to solve the case, but her descriptions of Laci's body being submerged in water in an area known for good fishing and the use of a home-made cement anchor to weigh it down both proved scarily accurate. Scott Peterson was convicted of murder and sentenced to death. He served eighteen years on death row before his sentence was commuted to life imprisonment in 2020 and is currently requesting a new trial based on a claim of jury misconduct.

Two of Renier's other high-profile cases were the disappearance of Natalee Holloway and the murder of JonBenét Ramsey...two cases I covered briefly in *The Dark Side of Humanity: True Crime Stories To Curl Up With*.

But let's discuss Gerard Croiset, a Dutch parapsychologist and psychic who gained international acclaim for his supposed ability to solve crimes, also using psychometry. Unfortunately, his successes were very limited. Perhaps his most famous case that he *didn't* solve is that of the missing Beaumont children.

Jane, Arnna, and Grant disappeared from Gleneig Beach near Adelaide, South Australia on January 26, 1966. Police investigations later revealed that, on the day of their disappearance, several witnesses saw the three children in the company of a tall man with light-brown to blond hair and a gaunt face with a tanned complexion. He had a medium build and was perhaps in his mid-thirties. Confirmed sightings of the children occurred at the Colley Reserve and at Wenzel's cake shop on Moseley Street, Glenelg. Despite numerous searches, however, neither the children nor their suspected companion were ever located.

The case received worldwide attention and is credited with causing a change in Australian lifestyles, since parents began to believe that their children could no longer be presumed to be safe when unsupervised in public.

On November 8, 1966, the Dutch psychic was brought to Australia to assist in the search, causing an absolute media storm. Croiset's efforts proved unsuccessful, with his story changing day-to-day and offering no clues. He did identify a spot at a warehouse near the children's home, where he believed their bodies had been buried inside an old brick kiln. The property owners, reluctant to excavate based only on a psychic's claim, soon bowed to public pressure after publicity helped raise $40,000 to have the building demolished. No remains, nor any evidence tied to any members of the Beaumont family, were found. In 1996, the building identified by Croiset was undergoing partial demolition and the owners allowed for a full search of the site. Once again, no trace was found of the children.

Nancy Myer is another notable psychic detective.

One of Nancy's most famous cases occurred in the early 2000s when she was called upon to assist in the search for a missing teenager in her hometown. Using her psychic abilities, Nancy provided law enforcement with crucial information that ultimately led to the discovery of the teenager's whereabouts, bringing closure to her family and friends.

But Nancy's talents extend beyond just locating missing persons. She has also provided valuable insights into cold cases, offering fresh perspectives and uncovering new leads that have reignited investigations long thought to be unsolvable.

Despite facing skepticism and criticism from some quarters, Nancy remains dedicated to using her gifts to help others. She continues to work tirelessly on behalf of law enforcement agencies and individuals seeking answers, offering hope and comfort to those affected by unsolved mysteries.

Nancy Myer's story serves as a testament to the power of the human spirit and the extraordinary potential of the mind. No matter if you believe in psychic abilities or not, there's no denying the impact that Nancy and other psychic detectives like her have had on the world of law enforcement and the lives of those they have helped.

REMOTE-VIEWING EXPERIMENTS

Remote-viewing experiments have long been a

subject of fascination for lovers of the obscure. These experiments involve individuals attempting to see or gather information about a distant or unseen target using extrasensory perception (ESP) or psychic abilities. The results of these experiments have been both intriguing and controversial, raising questions about the nature of reality and the limits of human perception.

In the realm of true paranormal unsolved mysteries, remote viewing experiments have been conducted in various forms and places. Some have been carried out in controlled laboratory settings, while others have taken place in more informal or spontaneous contexts. The results of these tests have varied widely, with some participants claiming to have successfully viewed distant locations or objects with remarkable accuracy, while another set reported mixed or inconclusive results.

Psychic phenomena and sensitivities play a central role in remote viewing experiments, as participants rely on their intuitive or extra-sensory abilities to access information beyond the limits of their physical senses. Some researchers believe that remote viewing may be a form of telepathy or clairvoyance, while others suggest that it may involve tapping into a collective or universal consciousness. Regardless of the underlying mechanism, remote viewing experiments continue to intrigue and challenge our understanding of the human mind and its potential capabilities.

Some participants of remote-viewing experiments have claimed to access information about long-lost civilizations, hidden treasures, or sought-after artifacts. It has raised questions about the origins of human civilization, the possibility of lost or forgotten knowledge, and the existence of advanced ancient technologies. While skeptics may dismiss these claims as mere speculation or wishful thinking, proponents of remote viewing argue that such experiments provide valuable insights into the mysteries of the past.

Perhaps one of the finest and well-known remote viewers is Major Ed Dames, a decorated Army man who worked as an operations and training officer for the Defense Intelligence Agency's top-secret Psychic Intelligence Unit. Together with his team, Dames used the practice of remote viewing to uncover accurate and verifiable military intelligence by going where nobody on the ground could go—into the enemy's mind.

After retiring, the major turned his paranormal detective skills to finding missing persons. He worked on cases such as the millionaire pilot Steve Fossett, whose plane vanished in Nevada, and a young Colorado girl named Christina White, who disappeared seemingly without a trace. He has even located a legendary missing object from history: the Ark of the Covenant.

In conclusion, remote viewing experiments, whether conducted in a laboratory setting or in the field, challenge our assumptions. For aficionados of the paranormal, remote viewing represents a fascinating frontier of exploration and discovery, inviting us to consider the possibility that the past may not be as distant or inaccessible as we once believed.

Chapter Four

Ancient Mysteries and Cryptic Codes

Ah, the enigmatic world of ancient mysteries and cryptic codes, where the echoes of the past reverberate through the corridors of time, dropping tantalizing clues. This chapter is an exploration into the depths of history, digging into some things that have captured the minds of generations. We work to unravel the mysteries that lie buried beneath the sands of time, seeking to unlock the cryptic codes that have confounded scholars and adventurers for centuries. Let's delve into the ancient past, where legends intertwine with reality, and the truth awaits those brave enough to uncover its hidden depths.

THE VOYNICH MANUSCRIPT

The Voynich Manuscript is among the most intriguing and mysterious artifacts in the field of paranormal investigations. Discovered in 1912 by Wilfrid Voynich, a Polish book dealer, this manuscript has baffled experts and researchers for centuries.

What sets the Voynich Manuscript apart from other ancient texts is the indecipherable nature of its language. Written in an unknown script and filled with strange illustrations of plants, animals, and celestial bodies, the Voynich Manuscript has been described as a "book that nobody can read." Countless cryptographers and linguists have attempted to crack its code, but all have met with frustration and failure. The script seems to defy any attempts at translation, leading to wild speculation about its origins and purpose.

Many theories abound, but none have been proven conclusively. Some believe it was created by an unknown Renaissance alchemist, while others think it may be a hoax designed to deceive future generations.

Another intriguing aspect of the document is its connection to psychic phenomena. Some researchers believe the manuscript may hold the key to unlocking psychic abilities or communicating with otherworldly beings. Others speculate that the strange symbols and illustrations contained within its pages may have been used in ancient rituals or ceremonies to harness supernatural forces.

Some experts believe the Voynich Manuscript may contain hidden knowledge about peoples long forgotten or advanced technologies. Others suggest that it could be a relic from a parallel universe or a message from extraterrestrial beings.

For lovers of the strange, the Voynich Manuscript is a tantalizing enigma that will forever capture the imagination. Whether it is a work of art, a scientific treatise, or a magical spellbook, the secrets of the Voynich Manuscript remain shrouded in mystery, waiting to be unraveled by those brave enough to dive into its cryptic pages.

THE ANTIKYTHERA MECHANISM

Let's take a peek at the perplexing tale of the Antikythera Mechanism—a relic that has left historians rubbing their chins for centuries.

It's the year 1901, and a group of sponge divers off the coast of the Greek island of Antikythera stumble upon something extraordinary—a corroded lump of bronze and wood buried beneath the ocean's depths.

At first glance, it looks like nothing more than a hunk of ancient debris. But upon closer inspection, archaeologists realize they've discovered something truly remarkable—the remains of a sophisticated mechanical device unlike anything seen before in the ancient world.

Dubbed the "Antikythera Mechanism," the ancient artifact is believed to date back to the first century BCE, making it over two thousand years old. The mind-boggling bit? The Antikythera Mechanism isn't just any old relic... It's a complex astronomical calculator, a marvel of ancient engineering that seems far ahead of its time.

The device consists of a series of interlocking gears and dials, meticulously crafted to track the movements of celestial bodies, predict eclipses, and even calculate the positions of the planets. In other words, it's essentially an ancient Greek analog computer, capable of performing complex astronomical calculations with astonishing precision.

But how did the ancient Greeks, with their rudimentary technology, manage to create such a sophisticated device? And what was its purpose? Some experts believe the Antikythera Mechanism was used for navigational or astronomical purposes, while others speculate that it may have had religious or astrological significance.

Despite decades of study and analysis, many questions about the Antikythera Mechanism remain unanswered. How did it end up at the bottom of the sea? Who built it, and why? And perhaps most baffling of all—how did the ancient Greeks possess the knowledge and technology to create such a marvel?

The Antikythera Mechanism is a baffling and intriguing subject that fascinates researchers to this day, serving as a tantalizing reminder of the ingenuity and intellect of our ancient ancestors. As we continue to unravel its mysteries, one thing's for sure—the Antikythera Mechanism will forever hold a special place in the chronicles of history, a testament to the enduring allure of the unknown.

THE LOST CITY OF ATLANTIS

Get ready for a deep dive into one of the finest tantalizing mysteries of all time—the lost city of Atlantis.

Legend has it that Atlantis was a thriving, advanced civilization, located somewhere beyond the Pillars of Hercules—what we now know as the Strait of Gibraltar. According to the ancient Greek philosopher Plato, who first wrote about Atlantis around 360 BCE, this mighty civilization was ruled by a powerful king named Atlas and was renowned for its wealth, technology, and military prowess.

According to Plato's accounts, Atlantis was struck by a catastrophic event—a series of earthquakes and floods that submerged the entire island beneath the sea in a single day and night. The once-great civilization was lost to the depths, nothing but speculation and intrigue remaining.

For centuries, scholars, explorers, and treasure hunters have searched in vain for the fabled city of Atlantis, scouring the oceans and combing the shores of distant lands in search of clues. Some believe Atlantis was a real place, lost to history but waiting to be rediscovered, while others dismiss it as nothing more than a myth or allegory.

Despite the lack of concrete evidence, numerous theories abound about the possible location of Atlantis. Some suggest that it may have been located in the Mediterranean Sea, near the island of Santorini, which was devastated by a volcanic eruption around 1600 BCE. Others propose more far-flung locations, such as the Caribbean, Antarctica, or even beneath the ice of the North Pole.

One of the most interesting aspects of the Atlantis legend is its enduring influence on popular culture and the human imagination. From novels and movies to video games and theme park attractions, Atlantis continues to capture the hearts and minds of people around the world, inspiring countless tales of adventure and exploration.

Whether Atlantis was a real place or just a product of ancient imagination may never be known for certain. But it is definitely a compelling and enigmatic legend that will likely endure for all time.

THE PLAIN OF JARS

Are you ready for a journey into the mysterious and enigmatic world of the Plain of Jars?

Located in the Xieng Khouang province of Laos, the Plain of Jars is an archaeological site unlike any other. Spread across the landscape are thousands of ancient stone jars, ranging in size from just a few feet to over ten feet tall, with some weighing several tons. These jars are thought to date back to the Iron Age, between 500 BCE and 500 CE.

But here's the intriguing part. No one knows for sure who built the jars or why. There are numerous theories, of course. Some believe they were used as burial vessels, while others suggest they may have been used for storing food or water. But the truth remains elusive, buried beneath the sands of time.

Adding to the mystery is the fact that the Plain of Jars has never been fully excavated. The area was heavily bombed during the Vietnam War, depositing unexploded ordnance that makes excavation dangerous and difficult. As a result, much of the site remains unexplored, its secrets waiting to be uncovered by fearless archaeologists.

The Plain of Jars baffles with its connection to ancient legends and folklore. Local myths tell of a race of giants who once roamed the land, using the jars as drinking vessels. Others speak of a great battle between rival kingdoms, with the jars serving as weapons or markers of victory.

Despite many, many years of research and speculation, the Plain of Jars continues to puzzle researchers and ignite the fire of those who dare to ponder its mysteries. Who built the jars, and why? What purpose did they serve, and what secrets do they hold? The answers may lie buried beneath the earth, waiting to be excavated by those daring enough to seek them out.

THE PARACAS CANDELABRA

Let's talk about a massive geoglyph etched into the side of a hill overlooking the Pacific Ocean in Peru.

Imagine yourself standing on the sandy shores of the Paracas Peninsula, gazing up at the towering cliffs that rise above the coastline. Suddenly, you spot it—a colossal figure carved into the earth, measuring over six hundred feet in length and visible from miles away. This is the Paracas Candelabra, named for its resemblance to a large candlestick.

The origins of the Paracas Candelabra are shrouded in mystery, with no definitive explanation for its creation or purpose. Carved into the desert floor over two thousand years ago, the geoglyph predates even the famous Nazca Lines—which I cover later—and shares similarities with other ancient geoglyphs found throughout the region.

But who created the Paracas Candelabra, and why? That's where the speculation begins. Similar to Nazca, some believe it was made by the ancient Paracas culture for religious or ceremonial purposes, while others wonder if it may have served as a navigational marker for sailors traversing the treacherous waters off the coast.

Interestingly enough, the Paracas Candelabra bears a striking resemblance to other geoglyphs found in distant lands, leading to speculation about possible connections between ancient civilizations. Some even propose more outlandish theories, suggesting that the geoglyph may have been created by extraterrestrial beings.

Despite many years of research and analysis, the true purpose of the Paracas Candelabra remains unknown. Its enigmatic presence continues to captivate the imagination of researchers, adventurers, and conspiracy theorists alike, inviting speculation and wonder about the mysteries of the ancient world.

As you stand in awe before the towering figure of the Paracas Candelabra, you can't help but wonder—what secrets lie buried beneath its sandy surface? Perhaps one day, the answers will be revealed, unlocking the secrets of this ancient formation and shedding light on the enduring legacy of the Paracas culture. But until then, the Paracas Candelabra remains a silent sentinel, standing watch over the windswept shores of Peru and guarding its secrets for eternity.

SACSAYHUAMÁN

Let's take a journey. We're still in Peru, wandering through the highlands, surrounded by breathtaking mountain scenery and ancient ruins at every turn. Suddenly, you stumble upon it—a massive fortress-like structure made up of gigantic stone blocks, each one meticulously carved and fitted together like a giant jigsaw puzzle. This, my friends, is Sacsayhuamán.

Located just outside the city of Cusco, Sacsayhuamán is a UNESCO World Heritage Site and among the most impressive examples of Inca architecture in the world. But it's kind of mind-blowing. The stones used to build Sacsayhuamán are absolutely massive, some weighing upwards of two hundred tons, and they fit together so perfectly that not even a blade of grass can slip between them.

Now, you might be thinking, *"How on earth did the ancient Incas manage to move and carve these behemoths without modern technology?"* And trust me, you're not alone in wondering that. Archaeologists and historians have been wracking their brains to come up with options for how Sacsayhuamán came to be for centuries, and the truth is, we still don't have all the answers.

Some theories suggest that the Incas used ramps, pulleys, and sheer manpower to transport and position the stones, while others propose more mystical explanations involving levitation or extraterrestrial assistance. And then there are those who believe that Sacsayhuamán wasn't just a fortress, but a sacred ceremonial site with spiritual significance.

The mysterious energy of Sacsayhuamán is fascinating. Visitors to the site often report feeling a sense of awe and wonder, as if they're tapping into something ancient and otherworldly. Some even claim to have had paranormal experiences while exploring the ruins, further adding to its mystique.

So, if you're a history buff, an adventure seeker, or just someone with a curious mind, Sacsayhuamán is a must-visit destination that will leave you pondering the buried questions and hidden answers of the long-ago past, well after you've returned home. Who knows what secrets lie hidden within its ancient stones? Only one way to find out—go see for yourself!

CLEOPATRA'S TOMB

Here's a story that's equal parts history, intrigue, and ancient legend.

Cleopatra—you've probably heard of her, right? The legendary queen of Egypt, famous for her beauty, intelligence, and scandalous love affairs with Julius Caesar and Mark Antony?—has a really juicy story. When Cleopatra died in 30 BCE, the location of her tomb became one of the greatest unsolved mysteries of the ancient world.

According to historical accounts, Cleopatra was buried alongside Mark Antony in a grand mausoleum somewhere in Alexandria, Egypt. But despite centuries of searching, her final resting place has never been definitively found.

Some believe that Cleopatra's tomb lies hidden beneath the streets of modern-day Alexandria, buried under layers of sand and debris. Others speculate that it may have been destroyed or looted in the chaos that followed her death, with nothing but scattered remnants and lost treasures left behind.

And then the story takes a paranormal twist. Legend has it that Cleopatra's tomb is cursed, guarded by restless spirits and ancient hexes that deter anyone foolish enough to seek it out. Tales of mysterious deaths, strange sightings, and things that just can't be explained have surrounded the search for Cleopatra's tomb for centuries, leaving archaeologists and treasure hunters alike wary of delving too deeply into the mysteries that lie in the depths of history.

Despite the dangers and uncertainties, the quest for Cleopatra's tomb endures, compelling adventurers and historians around the world. Will her final resting place ever be found? Or will Cleopatra's tomb remain forever lost to the sands of time, a tantalizing enigma that refuses to yield its secrets? Regardless, the story of Cleopatra's tomb is far from over, and the truth may be stranger than fiction.

THE YONAGUNI MONUMENT

Buckle up for a dive into the mysterious depths of the ocean and the engrossing tale of the Yonaguni Monument—a mind-blowing underwater structure off the coast of Japan.

Say you're out for a leisurely dive in the crystal-clear waters of the East China Sea when suddenly, out of nowhere, you stumble upon what appears to be a massive, man-made structure rising up from the ocean floor. And no, your eyes aren't playing tricks on you—that's the Yonaguni Monument, a colossal rock formation that looks like something straight out of an ancient civilization's playbook.

And the Yonaguni Monument is unlike anything else

found in the surrounding area. Carved out of solid rock, it features sharp, angular edges, perfectly straight lines, and even what appear to be staircases and terraces. Some researchers believe that the monument may be over ten thousand years old, predating even the Egyptian pyramids.

But there's more. No one is sure how the Yonaguni Monument came to be or what purpose it served. Some speculate that it may have been built by an ancient civilization as a ceremonial site or religious temple, while others offer up more outlandish theories involving extraterrestrial visitors or lost civilizations—because isn't it always?

The Yonaguni Monument lies at the center of a region known for its seismic activity, leading some researchers to suggest that it may have been shaped by natural geological processes rather than human hands. But even if that's the case, it still doesn't explain the monument's uncanny resemblance to man-made structures.

And then there's the paranormal aspects. Some divers and researchers who have explored the Yonaguni Monument report feeling strange sensations and experiencing things that can't be explained while in its vicinity. From mysterious lights and sounds to feelings of unease and discomfort, the monument seems to have a reputation for giving people the heebie-jeebies.

So, whether you're a seasoned diver, an armchair archaeologist, or someone with a healthy dose of curiosity, the Yonaguni Monument is a must-see relic that will leave you pondering the mysteries of the deep for years to come. What secrets lie hidden beneath the waves?

STONEHENGE

Picture wandering through the rolling hills of Wiltshire, England, when suddenly, rising up before you like a giant puzzle, you see it—Stonehenge. And no, I'm not talking about some run-of-the-mill collection of boulders. I'm talking about a massive stone circle, made of gigantic slabs arranged in a mysterious formation that's left historians with more questions than answers for centuries.

But Stonehenge isn't just any old pile of rocks. It's a marvel of ancient engineering, with some of the stones weighing upwards of twenty-five tons and standing over twenty feet tall. And get this, some of the stones were transported from quarries over one hundred miles away, a feat that boggles the mind when you consider that this was all done without any modern machinery or technology.

No one knows why Stonehenge was built or what purpose it served. Like most natural wonders, some theories suggest that it was a religious site, used for ceremonies and rituals by the ancient people who built it. Others propose more practical explanations, such as an astronomical observatory or a burial ground for important figures.

What about those who believe that Stonehenge may have had a more supernatural purpose? From ley lines and energy vortexes to theories about alien visitors or lost civilizations, the possibilities are as endless as they are tantalizing.

Stonehenge's enduring allure is captivating. Despite centuries of study and speculation, it is one of the greatest unsolved mysteries of ancient times, inviting us to ponder the secrets of our distant past and the enigmatic forces that shaped our world.

If you're a history buff, someone with a sense of wonder, or both, Stonehenge is a great place to visit. Imagine the secrets hidden within its ancient stones. Maybe I'll be able to tell you more after I visit soon...

THE CORAL CASTLE

I'm going to wrap up this chapter with a story close to home for me. And get ready for a wild ride. This is the story of a mind-boggling monument built entirely by one man, using nothing but sheer determination, ingenuity, and a whole lot of mystery.

In Homestead, Florida, there is an open-air *castle* made entirely out of coral rock—massive megalithic structures, towering walls, and intricate sculptures that seem to defy the laws of physics. Entire rooms built from the coral rock, complete with bathtub, bed, and more.

And the whole shebang was built by one guy, a Latvian immigrant named Edward Leedskalnin, who supposedly single-handedly carved and sculpted over eleven hundred tons of coral rock to create his own personal masterpiece.

But no one can say how Ed managed to pull off this incredible feat. He was notoriously secretive about his methods, claiming that he had discovered the secrets of the ancient Egyptians and used them to levitate and move the massive stones. Not to mention, he was only five feet tall!

And if that's not enough to make your head spin, get this—some people believe Ed had some kind of supernatural abilities or paranormal powers that allowed him to manipulate the stones with his mind. Others speculate that he may have had help from extraterrestrial beings or tapped into some kind of mystical energy source. After all, every morning, more and more of the structure would be constructed, defying all rational explanations.

But regardless of how he did it, the Coral Castle remains one of Florida's greatest unsolved mysteries, leaving visitors pondering its origins and wondering just how one man managed to build such an incredible monument with nothing but his own two hands and a whole lot of determination.

I visited and can tell you firsthand that the energy of that place is unlike anything I've ever experienced before. I'm a certified spiritual intuitive and a paranormal investigator and the draw of the site was utterly compelling. I didn't want to leave, and every pain I had before entering that fenced-off area disappeared. It sort of reminded me of Sedona, Arizona. Which makes me wonder if there are ley lines and/or vortexes on that piece of south Florida land. Intuition says yes.

The Coral Castle is a must-see destination for anyone interested in the weird and wonderful world of the paranormal. Maybe you should check it out for yourself and join me in wondering what the inspiration was that could cause a man to spend twenty-eight years carving a coral castle from the ground up, using nothing but homemade tools.

Was it unrequited love? Billy Idol wrote his famous song *Sweet Sixteen* about Ed's true story, wherein he was dumped by his fiancée Agnes Scuffs the day before they were to be married.

Perhaps it was to illustrate ancient sciences that defy gravity?

Or maybe just sheer, raw human determination.

Whatever it was, the Coral Castle is an everlasting mystery to those who explore it.

Chapter Five

Reincarnation and Past Lives

REINCARNATION IS a concept that has captivated cultures around the world for millennia. From ancient spiritual traditions to modern-day accounts of past-life memories, the tantalizing evidence and puzzling anecdotes that hint at the possibility of lives lived beyond our current existence is captivating. Let's see if we can get any answers to the age-old question: Is there life after death, and do we carry the echoes of our past lives within us?

CHILDREN WHO REMEMBER PAST LIVES

At the heart of paranormal occurrences and unsolved mysteries lies one intriguing phenomenon that has captured the attention of researchers and enthusiasts alike. The concept of children who remember past lives. These children, often very young, possess vivid memories of a life they supposedly lived before their current incarnation. These memories can be incredibly detailed and specific, providing information about places, people, and events that the child could not possibly have known through normal means.

Indescribable gifts are often attributed to these children who remember past lives. Many believe they possess a heightened psychic ability that allows them to access memories from past incarnations. Some researchers suggest the children may be reincarnated souls who have retained memories from their previous lives, while others believe that these memories are a form of genetic or ancestral memory passed down through generations.

Some scholars have suggested they may be able to provide valuable insights into historical events that have been lost to time. By studying the details of these past-life memories, researchers hope to uncover new evidence that could shed light on ancient mysteries and help us better understand the nature of human consciousness and existence.

One famous case of a child who remembered a past life is that of James Leininger, a young boy who claimed to be a World War II pilot named James Huston, Jr. James was able to provide detailed information about Huston's life and the aircraft carrier he served on, despite never having been exposed to the information before. His story has been extensively studied and documented, leading many to believe that there is indeed something extraordinary at play when it comes to children who remember past lives.

As lovers of true crime, paranormal occurrences, unsolved mysteries, and reincarnation, we are constantly seeking answers to the unexplainable and the supernatural. The stories of kids who remember past lives offer an interesting glimpse into the unknown arenas of the human mind and the nature of consciousness. By delving deeper into these cases and studying the evidence presented by these children, we may one day unlock the secrets of the past and gain a greater understanding of the mysteries that surround us.

THE CASE OF BRIDEY MURPHY

This is a tale that'll make you question everything you thought you knew about life, death, and the afterlife.

It's the 1950s, and a woman named Virginia Tighe is undergoing hypnosis therapy with a guy named Morey Bernstein. Nothing out of the ordinary, right? Well, hold on to your hat, because things are about to get really interesting.

Under hypnosis, Virginia starts spouting off details about her past life as a woman named Bridey Murphy, who supposedly lived in nineteenth-century Ireland. She rattles off all sorts of specifics—her address, her husband's name, even the name of her childhood sweetheart—all with the kind of confidence that would make anyone do a double-take.

Morey decides to do some digging and, lo and behold, he starts uncovering evidence that seems to corroborate Virginia's story. He finds records of a woman named Bridey Murphy Corkell, who lived in the same area of Ireland during the same time period. Suddenly, the whole thing blows up into a media frenzy.

Skeptics started poking holes in the story, questioning

the reliability of hypnosis as a tool for retrieving past-life memories and pointing out inconsistencies in Virginia's recollections. And let's not forget the fact that no one can definitively prove or disprove the existence of this supposed past life.

So, what's the deal with Bridey Murphy? Was she a real person who lived and breathed in nineteenth-century Ireland, or was she just a figment of Virginia's imagination under hypnosis? The truth may never be known for sure, but Bridey Murphy is a baffling and tantalizing mystery that will live on in the paranormal world—a famous and controversial case, both puzzling and fascinating.

INVESTIGATING REINCARNATION CLAIMS

Reincarnation is a concept that has fascinated humanity for centuries. The idea that our souls can be reborn into new bodies is both intriguing and mysterious. Let's delve a bit into the world of reincarnation claims and investigate the evidence behind these extraordinary stories.

For lovers of the weird and wonderful, the investigation into reincarnation claims is a thrilling journey into the unknown. From children who remember past lives with astonishing accuracy to adults who have vivid memories of historical events they could not have possibly experienced, the evidence for reincarnation is both compelling and perplexing.

In our exploration of reincarnation claims, we examine the cases of individuals who have displayed incomprehensible knowledge, skills, and memories that seem to defy rational explanation. Through interviews with experts in the field of parapsychology and past-life regression therapy, we seek to unravel the mysteries surrounding these extraordinary happenings.

Sensitivities play a significant role in many reincarnation claims. From telepathic communication with deceased loved ones to visions of past lives during altered states of consciousness, the supernatural elements of these stories add an extra layer of intrigue to our investigation.

THE POLLACK SISTERS

This is one of my favorite tales...

In the small town of Hexham in England, two girls named Jacqueline and Joanna Pollock lived with their devoutly religious family. One morning before church, the neighbor boy came running over to ask Ms. Pollack if he could walk with the six-year-old and the eleven-year-old to church. Knowing the rest of the family would be following shortly, and believing it to be absolutely safe, Jacqueline and Joanna's mother gave the okay.

On the way, talking and joking, the trio noticed a car barreling toward them, going much too fast in the residential area, and careening wildly. It was absolutely too late for any of them to do anything, and the car hit them head-on, killing Jacqueline and Joanna instantly and causing their friend Anthony to die not too long after—at just nine years old.

As expected, the incident was absolutely devastating

to not only the family but also the community. Particularly when they found out that the driver of the car was from the next town over.

The woman had just gone through a horrific divorce and was in the middle of a custody battle for her kids. She took an abhorrent number of over-the-counter painkillers and barbiturates and got behind the wheel. Some believe it was an accident on account of her inebriated state, others believe she hit the children intentionally in an if-I-can't-have-my-kids-nobody-should-have-kids way. The woman was eventually spirited away to a psychiatric hospital where I believe she lived out her days.

As if that weren't interesting enough, while the family was devoutly Catholic, Florence and John—Jacqueline and Joanna's parents—often argued about reincarnation. John absolutely believed in the phenomena, whereas Florence did not, and thought her husband's beliefs to be heresiac. It almost caused the end of their marriage.

But John remained staunch in his conviction. He was one hundred percent convinced that with the power of prayer, their daughters would be returned to them. And while it made him even more religious, the loss of their girls caused Florence to turn from her faith.

About a year later, Florence discovered she was pregnant. Up until the day she gave birth, they believed they were having a girl. There was only one heartbeat, the imaging only showed one fetus. So, imagine their surprise when she gave birth to two—identical twin girls.

Odd enough, but things get odder. Despite them

being identical, they had differing markings. Jennifer had a small birthmark on her hip, in the exact same spot and shape as her older sister Jacqueline had. And Gillian had a white mark on her forehead that looked an awful lot like the scar Joanna had from the time she fell and hit her head on a bucket. It defied explanation. Identical twins generally share birthmarks and such...

But the weirdness didn't stop there.

When the twins were three months old, the family relocated to Whitley Bay, a town east of Hexham.

As the girls got older, it became disturbingly clear that Gillian and Jennifer seemed to remember Hexham in great detail, despite not having grown up there.

When the family returned to Hexham when the girls were about four, the twins pointed out and named landmarks they had never seen before, such as the school Joanna and Jacqueline had attended, the Hexham abbey, and a park their deceased sisters loved. The pair even seemed to know the way to the playground without having ever seen it.

The girls were also able to correctly separate and name toys that belonged to their older sisters—or them in their former lives, if you believe. They even had night terrors about being run over by a car. On one instance, Florence walked in on the girls, Gillian holding

Jennifer's head in her lap, stroking her sister's hair, telling her it would be okay, and saying her eyes were bleeding...the girl was fine.

It became obvious to John and Florence that Jennifer was Jacqueline and Gillian was Joanna. Jennifer was even dependent on Gillian because Joanna had been five years older than Jacqueline.

Then, all of a sudden, everything changed. When the girls turned five, the memories of their past lives just… faded away.

Some say the girls were just unfathomably smart and absorbed all the things their parents said about their sisters and their old home. Others absolutely believe that the souls of the girls' sisters had come to reside in their bodies. What do you think?

Chapter Six

Unsolved Archaeological Anomalies

Is THERE anything more interesting than the uncharted territories of the archaeological world, where the past meets the paranormal and the answers may lie hidden beneath the sands of time? Okay, maybe. But these are still fun.

THE STONE SPHERES OF COSTA RICA

An ancient and perplexing mystery...

Say you're wandering through the dense jungles of Costa Rica, surrounded by towering trees and the sounds of exotic wildlife. And, suddenly, you stumble upon them —gigantic stone spheres, scattered throughout the landscape like something out of a lost civilization's playground. What would you do?

The spheres aren't just any old rocks, though. They're perfectly carved and polished, some as small as a few inches in diameter, while others are massive, weighing several tons and standing over six feet tall.

And no one knows for sure who made them or why. The Indigenous people of Costa Rica have legends about the spheres being created by gods or ancient warriors, but the truth remains shrouded in mystery.

Some theories suggest the stone spheres were used for astronomical or navigational purposes, while a few propose more mystical explanations involving energy vortexes or ancient rituals. And then there are those who believe that the spheres may have been created by an advanced civilization that predates the arrival of the Spanish conquistadors.

Adding to the allure is the fact that the stone spheres are found in clusters throughout the country, with some arranged in geometric patterns or aligned with the movements of the sun and stars. And despite all the work put in, no one has been able to definitively explain how they were made or what they were meant to be used for.

Regardless of if you're a history buff, an amateur archaeologist, or just someone with a sense of wonder, you'll be left pondering the what's what of the Stone Spheres of Costa Rica.

THE NAZCA LINES

Imagine soaring high above the arid plains of the Nazca Desert, and you'll see them—gigantic figures, geometric shapes, and intricate patterns etched into the earth with stunning precision. These are the Nazca Lines, created by the ancient Nazca culture between 500 BCE and 500 CE.

Many of these geoglyphs are so large and intricate

that they can only be fully appreciated from the air. Some stretch for hundreds of feet, depicting animals such as birds, monkeys, and spiders. Others form geometric shapes and lines that seem to stretch to the horizon.

So, how did the ancient Nazca people create these remarkable works of art? That's where the mystery deepens. Despite centuries of study and speculation, not one person knows for sure how the Nazca Lines were created or what purpose they served.

Some theories suggest the Nazca people used simple tools such as wooden stakes and ropes to create the lines, and some theorize more elaborate techniques involving surveying equipment and mathematical calculations. But given the immense scale and complexity of the geoglyphs, many researchers remain baffled by their construction.

Then there's the fact that many of the Nazca Lines align with celestial events, such as the solstices and equinoxes, leading some to believe that they may have served as an astronomical calendar or religious symbols. Others speculate that they may have been used for ceremonial purposes or as markers for underground water sources.

You can't help but respect the enigmatic nature of the Nazca Lines. Despite centuries of study and analysis, they continue to defy easy explanation, leaving only a legacy of wonder that captivates the imagination of people around the world.

Whether the Nazca Lines were created for practical, religious, or ceremonial purposes may never be known for certain. But their mysterious beauty and ancient allure

will continue to inspire awe and wonder for generations
to come.

THE MYSTERY OF THE CRYSTAL SKULLS

The mystery of the crystal skulls has fascinated
believers in the paranormal and skeptics alike for
centuries. These mysterious artifacts, often made of
quartz crystal and intricately carved into human skulls,
are said to hold powerful spiritual energy and ancient
wisdom. Many believe that the crystal skulls are
connected to ancient civilizations such as the Mayans,
Aztecs, and even the lost city—or continent, if you believe
it was bigger as some do—of Atlantis.

An often documented crystal skull is the Mitchell-
Hedges Skull, discovered by British explorer F.A.
Mitchell-Hedges in the 1920s in Belize. This skull is
believed to be thousands of years old and is said to have
supernatural powers, including the ability to heal and
communicate with the spirit world. Despite numerous
scientific tests, the origins and purpose of the Mitchell-
Hedges Skull remain a mystery.

Another intriguing aspect of the crystal skulls is the
legend that they are connected to past lives and reincarnation. Some believe that those who are drawn to the
crystal skulls have a deep spiritual connection to them
from a previous life. This theory is supported by the fact
that many people report feeling a strong sense of famil-
iarity and connection when they come into contact with
the crystal skulls.

Psychics and mediums have long been drawn to the

skulls, claiming that they have the ability to channel ancient wisdom and unlock hidden truths. Some believe that they are a form of psychic technology that can enhance abilities and connect individuals to higher spiritual realms. Others believe the skulls are simply powerful tools for meditation and spiritual growth. I can tell you firsthand that being surrounded by crystal skulls during meditation is a transformative experience and something I highly recommend.

However, despite the skepticism surrounding the crystal skulls, their enigmatic presence prevails, gripping the minds of believers and researchers alike. Whether they are ancient artifacts imbued with mystical powers or elaborate hoaxes crafted by skilled artisans, the mystery of the crystal skulls remains unsolved. Whether their power is legit or psychosomatic, we can't ignore it. And even as we dive deeper into the realms of the supernatural and ancient mysteries, the crystal skulls stand as a testament to the enduring power of the human imagination and our fascination with the unknown.

THE TERRACOTTA ARMY

This is a wild one. Prepare to be transported back in time to ancient China, where a engrossing tale unfolds—the story of the Terracotta Army, a hauntingly beautiful marvel of the old world.

Our journey begins in the third century BCE, in the heart of the Qin Dynasty. Emperor Qin Shi Huang, a ruler known for his ambition and ruthlessness, sought to conquer not just the land of China, but also the afterlife itself. Believing in the existence of a vast underworld, he ordered the construction of a massive mausoleum to serve as his eternal resting place.

But Emperor Qin's mausoleum was no ordinary tomb. No, it was a sprawling necropolis filled with all the treasures and luxuries he had enjoyed in life, as well as a vast army of terracotta warriors—thousands upon thousands of life-sized soldiers, each one meticulously crafted and painstakingly painted to resemble the warriors of Qin's army.

As the years passed, the mausoleum remained hidden beneath the earth, its secrets guarded by the passage of time. But in 1974, a group of farmers stumbled upon the site while digging a well, and what they uncovered would send shockwaves through the archaeological world.

For there, beneath the soil, lay the Terracotta Army— a ghostly legion of soldiers frozen in time, their eyes staring blankly ahead, their weapons poised for battle. It was a sight to behold, both mesmerizing and chilling, as if the warriors themselves had risen from the dead to guard their emperor for all eternity.

But as archaeologists began to excavate the site, they uncovered something even more unsettling—a series of mysterious pits filled with the remains of horses, chariots, and other offerings, all seemingly placed there to accompany the emperor on his journey to the afterlife.

And that's not all. Legend has it that Emperor Qin's tomb is booby-trapped with deadly pitfalls and curses, designed to thwart would-be grave robbers and protect the treasures within. Some say that those who dare to disturb the emperor's slumber are fated to suffer.

Today, the Terracotta Army stands as a testament to the power and ambition of one of China's most infamous rulers, as well as a haunting reminder of the mysteries that rest beneath the earth.

Chapter Seven

Paranormal Investigations

THE WARRENS AND THEIR HAUNTED MUSEUM

Let's be real. In the field of paranormal science, few names hold as much weight as Ed and Lorraine Warren. Renowned for their work in the field of demonology and supernatural occurrences, the Warrens were pioneers in their time—and they're personal heroes of mine. One of the best things they worked on was the infamous haunted museum they curated, filled with artifacts and objects that were said to be portals for dark entities.

Closed to the public in 2019, the Warrens' haunted museum was a place like no other, jam-packed with afflicted relics and cursed items they collected over the years. From haunted dolls to possessed paintings, each object had its own chilling backstory, leaving visitors feeling uneasy. Many claimed to have experienced supernatural phenomena while inside the museum, with some even reporting being physically attacked by unseen forces.

Of course, among the most well-known objects in the Warrens' collection was the Annabelle doll, a Raggedy Ann that is said to be possessed by a malevolent spirit. The Warrens claimed the doll was responsible for a series of unexplainable events, including physical harm to those who dared to mock or disrespect it. Despite skepticism from some, many believed in the doll's dark powers and feared what it could do. There was even a series of movies made about her.

The Warrens' haunted museum became a hotbed of paranormal activity over the years, with visitors flocking from all over to experience the haunted items and the energy for themselves. Some claimed to have seen mists and orbs—some in humanoid shapes—heard disembodied voices, or felt sudden drops in temperature while inside the museum. The Warrens themselves often spoke of feeling the presence of malevolent entities lurking in the shadows, always watching and waiting.

The Warrens' haunted museum is—and will probably always be—a mystery, with many questions left unanswered. Some believe the objects housed within its walls still hold the power to influence the living, and then there are those who dismiss it as mere superstition. Regardless, the legacy of Ed and Lorraine Warren and their haunted museum lives on, snagging the hearts and minds of lovers of the supernatural.

Today, closed over zoning violations from the traffic the museum conjured—pun intended—the museum was disbanded and turned into a residential house. In 2022, some of the relics were moved out of the basement and taken on tour for a paranormal convention.

Makes you wonder if moving the haunted objects and taking them places to be ogled and ridiculed is a good idea, doesn't it? I'm not sure I would have done that. I barely made it past my meeting with Robert the Doll in Key West. I'm not sure I've ever been so polite...

GHOST-HUNTING TELEVISION

You know, there's something undeniably compelling about curling up on the couch with a bowl of popcorn and diving headfirst into the world of ghost-hunting television shows. From the spine-tingling encounters to the heart-pounding investigations, these shows have a way of sucking you in and leaving you glued to the screen, no matter how much your rational mind tells you to look away.

Take *Ghost Adventures*, for example. Hosted by Zak Bagans and his crew of fearless investigators, this show has become a staple of the paranormal television landscape. With its dramatic reenactments—overly dramatic some might say—high-tech gadgets, and hair-raising encounters, *Ghost Adventures* has a way of making you feel like you're right there in the thick of the action, exploring haunted locations and uncovering the truth behind the legends. And while Zak has come under scrutiny in recent years, the longevity and popularity of the show has never waned. People even flock to his museum in Las Vegas.

Then there's *Ghost Hunters*, the OG of ghost-hunting shows. With its down-to-earth approach and emphasis on scientific investigation, *Ghost Hunters* has earned a loyal following over the years. Watching Jason Hawes and his team of seasoned ghost hunters sift through the evidence and debunk the hoaxes is like a masterclass in paranormal investigation—and let's be honest, who doesn't love a good debunking? Do we miss Grant, Amy, Adam, and some of the others? Of course, we do. But guess what. Most of them have their own shows and that just gives us more to love.

There are so many others, but let's not continue without chatting about my personal favorite, *Paranormal Lockdown*, where hosts Nick Groff and Katrina Weidman lock themselves inside some of the world's most haunted locations for seventy-two hours straight. Talk about commitment. With its immersive storytelling and jaw-dropping evidence, *Paranormal Lockdown* pulls you into the action with Nick and Katrina, letting you experience the terror firsthand. They even did a spin-off, *Paranormal Lockdown: UK*, which was equally as good and made me fall down a rabbit hole of research into those locations. I'm even signing at the haunted Shrewsbury Prison in November of 2024 and cannot wait. They've told me they're putting me in the most haunted cell. I'll have to chime back in whether I get any great evidence.

While the show is no more, you can see Nick on his other shows *Ghosts of Shepherdstown,* and his new series *Death Walker*.

Katrina went on to do a show with Ozzy Osborne's son, Jack, called *Portals to Hell*.

So, what is it about these shows that keeps us coming back for more? Maybe it's the thrill of the unknown, the excitement of exploring the seemingly unsolvable. Perhaps it's the sense of camaraderie and connection, knowing that we're all in this together, searching for answers in a world filled with mysteries.

Ghost-hunting television shows have carved out a special place in the world of paranormal unsolved mysteries, Even if you're struggling with which side of the fence you're on, there's something undeniably fascinating and satisfying about watching these fearless investigators brave the unknown in search of the truth. So, grab your EVP recorder, your flashlight, and your handy-cam, my friends, because the adventure is just beginning!

THE ENFIELD POLTERGEIST CASE

Let's dive into one of the more perplexing paranormal unsolved-mystery cases—the Enfield Poltergeist. Strap in because this one's a wild ride.

It's the late 1970s, and we're in a quiet suburb of North London. The Hodgson family, just your average bunch, finds themselves at the center of a paranormal storm when strange things start happening in their home. Objects flying through the air, furniture moving on its own, disembodied voices whispering in the darkness—it's enough to send shivers down your spine.

But it's not just any old haunting—this one's got all the makings of a classic poltergeist case. The Hodgson's youngest daughter, Janet, seems to be the epicenter of the activity, with her body contorting in unnatural ways and her voice taking on an otherworldly tone. It's like something straight out of a horror movie.

But before we go on, let's discuss what a poltergeist actually is...

Unlike traditional hauntings where the focus is on apparitions, shadows, or ghostly figures, poltergeist activity typically involves randomly moving objects, loud noises, and other disturbances. These phenomena often occur in a specific location, such as a home or building, and tend to center around a particular individual, often a teenager or young person.

Poltergeist activity can manifest in a variety of ways, including objects being thrown or levitated, doors slamming shut, lights flickering on and off, and mysterious voices or whispers. In some cases, individuals may also report feeling a sense of unease or being watched, as if an unseen presence is lurking nearby.

One of the distinguishing features of poltergeist phenomena is the apparent connection to the emotions or psychological state of the individuals involved, causing what some believe is unrealized psychokinesis. It's often theorized that the disturbances are somehow linked to the subconscious mind of a person experiencing stress, trauma, or emotional turmoil, although the exact nature of this connection remains a subject of debate among paranormal researchers.

So, back to our story. Enter Maurice Grosse and Guy Playfair, two intrepid investigators who take on the case with gusto. Armed with tape recorders, cameras, and an unshakable determination, they set out to uncover the truth behind the Enfield Poltergeist. And let me tell you, what they find is enough to make your hair stand on end.

Over the course of their investigation, Grosse and

Playfair witness some truly bizarre phenomena—furniture levitating, strange knocking sounds, and even full-blown apparitions appearing out of thin air. It was enough to make even the most hardened skeptic question their beliefs.

But they also caught the young girls doing things to fake the occurrences. Despite that, they believe that lots of the experiences were genuine, and Ed and Lorraine Warren concurred.

Perhaps the most disturbing aspect of the Enfield Poltergeist case is the way it seems to defy explanation. Despite the best efforts of skeptics and debunkers, the evidence just keeps piling up, leaving us wondering what in the world could be causing all the paranormal activity.

So, what's the deal with the Enfield Poltergeist? Was it all just an elaborate hoax cooked up by the Hodgson family, or was there something genuinely supernatural at play? We may never know for sure.

Chapter Eight

Conspiracies and Cover Ups in Paranormal Phenomena

THE MEN IN BLACK

If we were ranking the most compelling mysteries in the world of science fiction and fantasy, few entities are as enigmatic and feared as the Men in Black. But it's not fiction—or at least the people who have encountered them don't think so. These shadowy figures have been reported throughout history, appearing after encounters with UFOs, strange phenomena, and other strange events. Their appearance is often described as unsettling, with pale skin, dark suits, and an unnerving sense of authority. But who are the Men in Black, and what is their connection to the paranormal world?

Some believe that the Men in Black are government agents tasked with covering up evidence of extraterrestrial activity and other supernatural occurrences. They are said to visit witnesses of these events, intimidating them into silence and erasing any evidence of their experiences. Others claim that the Men in Black are actually aliens themselves, using human disguises to move among us undetected. Whatever their true nature, encounters with the Men in Black often leave witnesses feeling shaken and fearful.

One of the most cited cases involving the Men in Black occurred in the 1960s, when UFO researcher Albert Bender claimed to have been visited by three mysterious men who warned him to stop investigating flying saucers. Bender's story captivated the public and sparked widespread speculation about the true identity and purpose of the Men in Black. Despite the theories and conspiracies, their origins remain a mystery, with some believing them to be interdimensional beings or even time travelers from the future.

Despite their sinister reputation, not all encounters with the Men in Black are negative. Some witnesses report feeling a sense of peace and enlightenment after their interactions, leading to theories that the Men in Black may possess psychic abilities or other powers. Could it be that these mysterious figures are not simply enforcers of secrecy, but guardians of hidden knowledge and ancient mysteries?

As we dig more into the world of the Men in Black, we are forced to confront the limitations of our understanding of the paranormal. Are they simply a figment of our imagination, or do they hold the key to unlocking the secrets of the universe? Who knows? But the Men in Black will continue to haunt the fringes of our reality, challenging our perceptions and pushing the boundaries of what we thought possible.

. . .

Rayvn Salvador

PROJECT BLUE BOOK

Project Blue Book was a top-secret United States Air Force investigation into unidentified flying objects (UFOs) that ran from 1952 to 1969. The purpose of the project was to determine if UFOs posed a threat to national security and to scientifically analyze any potential sightings. Over the course of its existence, Project Blue Book investigated over twelve thousand UFO sightings, with the majority of them being classified as explainable phenomena such as weather balloons or aircraft.

Despite the majority of sightings being debunked, there were a small percentage of cases that remained unsolved. These cases, known as "unidentified" or "unknowns," continue to intrigue and mystify researchers and enthusiasts alike. Some of the most famous cases investigated by Project Blue Book include the 1964 Lonnie Zamora incident in Socorro, New Mexico, and the 1967 Malmstrom Air Force Base UFO incident in Montana.

Many skeptics believe that Project Blue Book was simply a cover-up for government experiments or military technology that was not yet publicly known. However, believers in the paranormal and UFO phenomena argue that the government was trying to suppress evidence of extraterrestrial visitations. The truth behind Project Blue Book remains a subject of debate and speculation to this day.

Despite whether you believe in UFOs and extraterrestrial life or not, the impact of Project Blue Book on popular culture and the public's perception of the unknown cannot be denied.

In conclusion, Project Blue Book is a intriguing chapter in the history of paranormal investigations and UFO sightings. The project's findings, both explained and unexplained, continue to shape our understanding of the mysterious and the baffling. For those of us invested in all things that defy explanation, the legacy of Project Blue Book is a fascinating topic to delve into the realms of the unknown.

THE ROSWELL INCIDENT

The Roswell Incident is at the top of the most infamous and hotly debated events in recent-ish history. In July 1947, an unidentified flying object (UFO) reportedly crashed near Roswell, New Mexico. The U.S. military initially claimed it was a weather balloon, but later changed their story to say it was a top-secret nuclear test surveillance balloon. However, many believe that the government covered up the truth about what *really* happened that fateful day.

The Roswell Incident is a fascinating and intriguing case to explore. The mystery surrounding the crash and the alleged recovery of alien bodies has captured the minds of people around the world for decades. Eyewitness accounts, government documents, and conspiracy theories all contribute to the mystique and intrigue of this unsolved paranormal phenomenon.

Intuitive abilities may play a role in unraveling the truth behind the Roswell Incident. Some psychics claim to have communicated with extraterrestrial beings connected to the crash, and others believe that the government is hiding evidence of alien life on Earth. The idea of psychic communication with otherworldly beings adds another layer of complexity to this already enigmatic case.

Ancient mysteries and archaeological anomalies could also shed light on the Roswell Incident. Some researchers speculate that the crash site may hold clues to ancient civilizations or lost technologies that could explain the presence of the UFO. The possibility of finding ancient artifacts or evidence of an advanced civilization at the crash site adds a new dimension to the investigation of this paranormal unsolved mystery.

The Roswell Incident remains a tantalizing enigma that captivates connoisseurs of true paranormal unsolved mysteries. The combination of eyewitness testimony, government cover-ups, psychic phenomena, and ancient mysteries make this case a perfect fit for people like us. As researchers continue to delve into the secrets of Roswell, the truth behind this iconic event may finally be revealed.

Chapter Nine

The Unexplained Powers of Psychics and Mediums

THE AMAZING RANDI CHALLENGE

If you're reading this book, then you've probably heard of The Amazing Randi Challenge. This infamous challenge was created by magician and skeptic James Randi, who offered a cash prize to anyone who could demonstrate paranormal abilities under scientific conditions. The challenge was designed to debunk claims extra-sensory perception and has become a cornerstone in the sphere of paranormal investigation.

For lovers of true paranormal unsolved mysteries, The Amazing Randi Challenge presents a unique opportunity to separate fact from fiction. Many claim to have psychic abilities or to possess powers, but few have been able to pass the rigorous scientific testing required to claim the cash prize. The challenge has become a hot topic of debate among those fascinated by the paranormal. Some view it as a necessary measure to weed out frauds and charlatans, and others see it as a barrier to true discovery.

For those intrigued by ancient mysteries and anthropological anomalies, The Amazing Randi Challenge offers a chance to explore the boundaries of what we know and what we don't know we know. The challenge has attracted a wide range of participants, from self-proclaimed psychics to amateur archaeologists, all seeking to prove the existence of phenomena beyond the realm of scientific explanation. While many have failed to meet the challenge's strict criteria, a few have managed to pass the tests and claim the cash prize, sparking further debate and speculation among believers and skeptics alike.

Despite its controversial nature, The Amazing Randi Challenge has had a significant impact on the world of paranormal investigation. The challenge has forced many self-proclaimed psychics and mediums to rethink their beliefs and practices, while also inspiring a new generation of skeptics and debunkers to question the validity of paranormal claims. If you're interested in exploring the boundaries of human knowledge and understanding, The Amazing Randi Challenge remains a compelling case study in the ongoing quest to uncover the truth behind the esoteric intricacies of what we, as humans, are capable of.

If you're looking for a thrilling and thought-provoking journey into the world of the unknown, consider delving into The Amazing Randi Challenge more and see where it takes you.

THE LONG ISLAND MEDIUM

Most of us have heard of The Long Island Medium. Known for her uncanny ability to chat with the spirits of the deceased, she has captivated audiences with her astonishing gifts. But who is this enigmatic figure, and how does she do what she does?

The Long Island Medium, whose real name is Theresa Caputo, first gained widespread recognition through her hit reality TV show of the same name. Week after week, viewers would watch in awe as she connected with the spirits of loved ones who had passed away, delivering messages of comfort and closure to those left behind. But her abilities go far beyond what is shown on television.

Many skeptics have tried to debunk Caputo's claims, but time and time again, she has proven herself to be the real deal. Through her unique blend of psychic intuition and mediumship, she is able to tune into the energy of the spirit world and relay messages from beyond the grave with astonishing accuracy.

But Caputo's talents don't stop at communicating with the dead. She is also known for her ability to tap into the past lives of her clients, uncovering long-buried memories and traumas that continue to affect them in the present. This aspect of her work has led many to believe that she possesses a rare gift of reincarnation, allowing her to access the memories and experiences of past lives.

There is no denying the impact that The Long Island Medium has had on the world. Her ability to bridge the gap between the living and the dead has brought comfort and closure to countless individuals, and her work still inspires awe and wonder in those who seek answers to life's greatest mysteries. The Long Island Medium may remain an enigma, but one thing is for certain—her gifts are unlike anything the world has ever seen.

THE CASE OF THE FOX SISTERS

In the mid-nineteenth century, three young sisters from upstate New York claimed to have the ability to talk with the dead. Their seances became wildly popular, attracting the attention of believers and skeptics alike. The sisters—Leah, Margaret, and Kate Fox—were hailed as mediums and became celebrities in the spiritualist movement.

The Fox Sisters' abilities were put to the test by scientists, journalists, and even famous figures like Abraham Lincoln. Despite facing scrutiny and accusations of fraud, the sisters continued to hold seances and communicate with spirits. The mysterious messages they received during their seances baffled even the most skeptical observers.

The women's fame eventually led to their downfall, as rumors of deception and manipulation began to circulate. In 1888, Margaret Fox admitted to using tricks to produce the rappings heard during their seances. The confession cast doubt on the authenticity of the sisters' abilities and raised questions about the nature of their paranormal experiences.

The case of the Fox Sisters remains a controversial and debated topic among paranormal enthusiasts and historians. Some believe that the sisters were genuine mediums who were unfairly discredited, while others see them as clever frauds who capitalized on the gullibility of their followers. Regardless of the truth behind their abilities and actions, the Fox Sisters' legacy will likely fascinate and intrigue for many years to come.

The story of the Fox Sisters also serves as a warning of the dangers of blind belief and the importance of critical thinking when examining paranormal phenomena. Their case highlights the fine line between faith and skepticism, and the difficulty of separating truth from fiction. Whether the sisters were genuine mediums or skilled charlatans, their story remains a compelling and enigmatic chapter in the history of the occult.

Chapter Ten

Supernatural Events and Haunted Objects

SOME OF THE most intriguing paranormal stories revolve around haunted objects—not people or locations. So, let's take a peek.

THE HOPE DIAMOND

Here, we journey to the depths of India, where a magnificent blue diamond eventually known as the Tavernier Blue was discovered in the seventeenth century. Legend has it this dazzling gem was extracted from the eye of a sacred idol by a cunning thief, setting off a chain of events that would change the course of history forever.

Enter Jean-Baptiste Tavernier, a French merchant who acquired the diamond and brought it back to Europe, where it caught the eye of none other than King Louis XIV of France. Enamored by its beauty, the king ordered the diamond to be recut into a magnificent gem that would come to be known as the Hope Diamond.

But little did King Louis know, the diamond carried with it a dark and sinister curse—one that would bring misfortune and tragedy to all who possessed it. From the moment the Hope Diamond entered the royal court, whispers of death and despair followed in its wake.

Over the centuries, the diamond passed through the hands of kings and queens, aristocrats and adventurers, each one falling victim to the curse that seemed to cling to the precious gem like a shroud of darkness. Some met untimely ends. Others suffered financial ruin or scandalous downfall—all attributed to the malevolent influence of the Hope Diamond.

The unexplained phenomena that seems to surround the diamond's history is surprising. From strange lights and noises to accidents and inexplicable deaths, the gem's presence has been linked to a litany of paranormal occurrences that defy rational explanation.

Today, the Hope Diamond resides in the Smithsonian Institution in Washington, D.C., where it continues to fascinate visitors with its haunting beauty.

If you ever find yourself in the presence of the Hope Diamond, tread carefully, my friends, for you may be tempting fate itself. For in the deeps of its azure depths lies a tale of darkness and despair—one that reminds us that even the most precious treasures can be tainted by the touch of the supernatural.

THE ANNABELLE DOLL

In the wide world of true crime, paranormal occurrences, and unsolved mysteries, Annabelle is a household name. This eerie tale has captivated audiences for years, sparking debates about the existence of reincarnation, the presence of diabolical influences, and the power of psychic phenomena. The storied history of the Annabelle doll is a haunting reminder that some mysteries may never be solved.

Annabelle first gained notoriety in the 1970s when a young woman named Donna received it as a gift from her mother. Strange things began happening almost immediately after the doll entered Donna's home. At first, it was small things like misplaced objects and random noises. But as time went on, Donna and her roommate Angie began to experience more sinister occurrences.

One night, Donna and Angie awoke to find the doll had moved on its own, seemingly changing positions while they slept. They also reported seeing the doll's expression change, as if it were alive. Terrified, the women sought the help of a psychic, who revealed that the doll was inhabited by the spirit of a young girl named Annabelle Higgins who had died tragically years before.

As the activity surrounding the Annabelle Doll escalated, the women knew they had to take action. They contacted renowned paranormal investigators Ed and Lorraine Warren, who confirmed that the doll was indeed possessed by a malevolent entity. The Warrens took the doll into their possession, but even they struggled to contain its dark energy.

The Annabelle Doll remains a source of fascination and fear for those who study true paranormal unsolved mysteries and probably always will. Some believe that the doll's power lies in its connection to ancient mysteries and archaeological anomalies. Another set attributes its haunting presence to the unfathomable powers of psychic phenomena or diabolical infestation. Whatever the truth may be, the story of the Annabelle Doll will continue to intrigue and terrify lovers of the supernatural for years to come. And I, for one, am here for it.

THE HAUNTED PAINTING OF *THE HANDS RESIST HIM*

The Haunted Painting of *The Hands Resist Him* is a gripping tale that has captured the attention of lovers of the weird—like us. This unnerving story revolves around a painting created by artist Bill Stoneham in 1972, titled *The Hands Resist Him*. The painting depicts a young boy standing next to a doll-like girl, both with lifeless eyes and hands reaching toward the viewer. The unsettling nature of the painting is just the beginning of the mystery that surrounds it.

Many who have made contact with the painting claim to have experienced strange phenomena. Some report feeling a sense of unease or dread when looking at the painting, and others claim to have seen the figures in the frame move. One particularly harrowing account comes from a couple who purchased the painting on eBay and claimed that the figures in the painting would sometimes disappear altogether, only to reappear in different positions later on.

Some psychics who have examined the painting believe that it is haunted by the spirits of the children depicted in it. Others believe that the painting acts as a portal to another dimension, allowing entities to pass through into our world. Whatever the case may be, there is no denying that there is something deeply unsettling about this piece of art.

The mystery of *The Hands Resist Him* deepens when considering the origins of the painting. Bill Stoneham has stated that he based the painting on a series of dreams he had as a child, in which he saw himself and a young girl trapped in a glass pane. Could these dreams be a glimpse into past lives or some other form of reincarnation? The connection between the artist, the painting, and the strange occurrences surrounding it only adds to the intrigue of this already enigmatic mystery.

As lovers of true paranormal unsolved mysteries, we cannot help but be drawn to the riddle of this story. The painting has captured the imaginations of many and continues to both intertest and terrify those who come into contact with it. it's sure to leave you questioning the boundaries between art, reality, and the supernatural.

JAMES DEAN'S CAR

This story might make you think twice about hopping behind the wheel...

In the 1950s, James Dean, Hollywood's rebel without a cause, was tearing up the streets in his sleek and iconic Porsche 550 Spyder. But little did he know, the car would become the stuff of legends—and nightmares.

You see, on a fateful day in 1955, James Dean met his

untimely end in a tragic car accident while driving his beloved Porsche. But there's more to the story. Legend has it the wreckage of Dean's car was salvaged and sold for parts, but the cursed vehicle had other plans.

In the years that followed, strange and inexplicable occurrences began to plague anyone who came into contact with the car—or even parts of it. Some say they heard ghostly whispers echoing from the twisted metal, other people claimed to see the ghostly figure of James Dean himself, still behind the wheel and speeding toward his doom.

And then there's the string of accidents and misfortunes that seemed to follow in the car's wake. From mysterious fires to inexplicable mechanical failures, it seemed as though the car was cursed, leaving a trail of destruction in its path.

Today, the remainder of the wreckage of James Dean's car sits in a museum, a grim reminder of the dangers of speed and recklessness. But some say that the car's malevolent presence still lingers, haunting anyone who dares to get too close.

So, when next you find yourself cruising down the highway, spare a thought for James Dean and his cursed Porsche. Who knows, you might just catch a glimpse of his ghostly figure in the rearview mirror, reminding you to drive safe and watch out for the things that go bump in the night.

THE KOH-I-NOOR DIAMOND

All right, folks, let me spin you a tale about one of the

world's most famous and most cursed gemstones—the Koh-i-Noor Diamond. This beauty has a history as rich and mysterious as the depths of the ocean, and trust me, it's not for the faint of heart.

Legend has it the Koh-i-Noor Diamond, which means "Mountain of Light" in Persian, was plucked from the eye of an ancient Hindu god and passed down through generations of rulers and conquerors. But with great beauty comes great danger, and the Koh-i-Noor Diamond has a reputation for bringing misfortune to all who possess it.

The diamond's tale takes us on a whirlwind journey through the annals of history, from the Mughal Empire to the British Crown. Each new owner of the Koh-i-Noor Diamond seemed to be cursed with tragedy and turmoil, as if the gemstone itself were imbued by some ancient power.

One of the most often told stories associated with the diamond is that of the British Empire, which acquired the Koh-i-Noor Diamond during the colonial era. But far from bringing glory and prosperity to the British Crown, the diamond seemed to bring nothing but trouble, with tales of wars, betrayals, and political intrigue swirling around it like a dark cloud.

But it's not just the diamond's owners who have felt its curse—those who have come into contact with the Koh-i-Noor Diamond have reported strange things, from nightmares and hallucinations to a sense of impending doom.

Today, the Koh-i-Noor Diamond resides in the Tower of London, where people can marvel at its dark and mysterious history. Some say that the diamond's curse still lingers, casting a shadow of fear and uncertainty over all who dare to gaze upon its glittering surface.

THE UNLUCKY MUMMY

This story isn't actually about a mummy but a coffin lid of a high-status woman who lived around 950-900 BCE. Discovered in Thebes in the 1800s, the four Englishmen who later purchased the lid all died in unfortunate circumstances.

Legend has it the mummy was cursed, its resting place disturbed by the hands of greedy tomb raiders. And from the moment it was unearthed, tragedy seemed to follow in its wake, as if the curse of the pharaohs had been unleashed upon the world once more.

One by one, those who encountered the sarcophagus lid met untimely ends—accidents, illnesses, and inexplicable deaths that defied rational explanation. Some say that the mummy itself was to blame, its malevolent spirit exacting revenge on all who dared to disturb its eternal slumber.

Despite the best efforts of scientists and skeptics to dismiss the curse as mere superstition, the evidence seemed to suggest otherwise—as if some unseen force was at work, punishing those who dared to defy the ancient gods.

In the early twentieth century, journalist William Thomas Stead wrote an article on the cursed object. Not long after, Stead was on the Titanic—and we all know how that ended. It is said he told stories of the mummy up to the ship's unfortunate disaster, and many today believe the curse may have been to blame for the ship's watery end.

Today, the Unlucky Mummy resides in a British museum, its dark reputation preceding it like a shadow of death. Visitors flock from far and wide to catch a glimpse of the cursed relic, drawn by the allure of the supernatural and the thrill of temptation.

ÖTZI

Okay, this is a fun one about one of history's most fascinating—and haunted—mysteries: the haunting of Ötzi the Iceman. Now, this isn't your typical ghost story, nor is it a haunted object, really—though I guess a man popsicle could be—but trust me, it's got all the makings of a spine-tingling tale.

Let me set the stage. It's the year 1991, and a couple of hikers are trekking through the Ötztal Alps along the border between Austria and Italy. Suddenly, they stumble upon something that sends shivers down their spines—a mummified corpse frozen in the ice, perfectly preserved for over five thousand years. That's right, folks, we're talking about Ötzi the Iceman.

Now, Ötzi's story is already fascinating enough on its own. He was a Copper Age wanderer who met his untimely demise high up in the Alps, likely due to foul play or a freak accident. But there's more, and it's even spookier.

You see, ever since Ötzi's mummified remains were discovered, people have reported a wide array of strange and inexplicable phenomena surrounding the ancient iceman. Some say they've heard disturbing whispers echoing through the mountains. Others claim to have seen Ötzi's ghost wandering the Alpine trails, his haunting gaze fixed on those who dare to cross his path.

But perhaps the most unsettling aspect of Ötzi's haunting is the string of misfortunes that seem to follow anyone who comes into contact with his remains. From sudden illnesses to freak accidents, it's as if Ötzi's curse knows no bounds, wreaking havoc on all who dare to disturb his eternal slumber.

Today, Ötzi's mummified remains are housed in a museum in Italy, where they continue to astonish visitors from around the world. Some say that Ötzi's spirit still roams the Alpine peaks, restless and vengeful, seeking retribution for the injustices done to him in life.

If you ever decide to hike the Ötztal Alps, keep an eye out for Ötzi the Iceman. You might just catch a glimpse of his ghostly figure lingering in the shadows, a reminder of the ancient mysteries that still haunt these rugged mountains to this day.

THE DYBBUK BOX

Let's go over the haunting of the Dybbuk Box. Now, you might be thinking, *What in the world is a Dybbuk Box?* Well, hold onto your hats because this story is about to get seriously creepy.

It all started back in 2001, when a man named Kevin Mannis bought an antique wine cabinet at an estate sale in Portland, Oregon. Little did he know, he was about to unleash a nightmare beyond his wildest imagination.

You see, this wasn't just any old wine cabinet—it was a Dybbuk Box, a type of haunted Jewish artifact said to contain an evil spirit known as a dybbuk. Legend has it that the dybbuk attaches itself to the box and brings misfortune and misery to anyone who dares to open it.

And boy, did Kevin Mannis learn that the hard way. From the moment he brought the Dybbuk Box into his home, strange and inexplicable things started happening. Lights flickered, objects moved on their own, and sinister whispers filled the air. It was like a horror movie.

But the terror didn't stop there. Mannis soon realized that he wasn't the only one affected by the Dybbuk Box—friends, family, and even complete strangers reported experiencing strange and unsettling phenomena whenever they came into contact with the cursed artifact.

In a desperate attempt to rid himself of the Dybbuk Box's malevolent influence, Mannis sold it to a series of unsuspecting buyers, each one falling victim to the box's curse in turn. It seemed as though the Dybbuk Box was unstoppable, leaving a trail of chaos and terror in its wake.

Today, the Dybbuk Box resides in the possession of Zak Bagans, host of the paranormal reality television series *Ghost Adventures*. But even now, its sinister presence lives on, haunting those who dare to come near it, serving as a reminder of the dangers that lurk in the darkness.

So, if you happen to stumble upon an antique wine cabinet at an estate sale, think twice before you open it.

You never know what malevolent forces might be lurking inside, waiting to unleash their wrath upon the unsuspecting souls who dare to disturb their slumber.

THE DEVIL'S ROCKING CHAIR

The story of David Glatzel and the Devil's Rocking Chair is an engaging tale that delves into the depths of the paranormal world, filled with eerie occurrences and unexplained phenomena.

It all began in 1980, when the Glatzel family moved into a rental property in Brookfield, Connecticut. Soon after settling in, they began experiencing strange and terrifying events. Objects would move on their own, strange noises echoed through the house, and an oppressive feeling of dread hung in the air.

But the most disturbing occurrences centered around the youngest member of the family, David Glatzel. David began experiencing vivid nightmares and claimed to see a terrifying demonic entity lurking in the shadows. He spoke of feeling a sinister presence, and his behavior grew increasingly erratic and aggressive.

Fearing for their son's safety, the Glatzel family reached out to a local couple, Ed and Lorraine Warren, renowned paranormal investigators. The Warrens conducted an investigation and concluded that David was indeed under attack by a malevolent entity.

As the haunting escalated, David's condition worsened. He began exhibiting signs of possession, speaking in strange voices and displaying superhuman strength. In a desperate attempt to rid David of the demoniacal presence, the Warrens enlisted the help of a Catholic priest, Father Raymond Bishop, to perform an exorcism.

During the exorcism, David allegedly levitated and spoke in tongues, and at one point, he even claimed to see the devil himself. The ordeal lasted for several hours, but eventually, the entity was expelled from David's body, and he returned to normal.

But that's not where the story ends. After the exorcism, the Warrens took possession of a rocking chair from the Glatzel's home, which was believed to be a focal point of the demonic activity. This chair, known as the Devil's Rocking Chair, became infamous in paranormal circles, with reports of strange phenomena continuing to surround it.

The Devil's Rocking Chair was in the Warrens' occult museum until Zak Baggans purchased it. Regardless of where it resides, it's a haunting reminder of the terrifying ordeal endured by the Glatzel family. The events of that fateful year continue to puzzle and intrigue paranormal enthusiasts, serving as a stark reminder of the power and malevolence of the supernatural world.

ROBERT THE DOLL

This story begins in the early twentieth century, in the sunny seaside town of Key West, Florida. In the grand Victorian mansion of the Otto family, young Robert Eugene Otto received a special gift from his family's Bahamian maid—an innocuous-looking doll, dressed in a sailor suit.

But this was no ordinary doll. Some say it was harmless and just somehow absorbed negative energy, and others believe the maid placed a curse on the doll as retribution for being let go from her position. Regardless, from the moment Robert laid eyes on his new toy, strange things began to happen. Rooms would inexplicably go cold, furniture would move on its own, and unnerving giggles would echo through the house in the dead of night.

As time went on, the Otto family grew increasingly unnerved by Robert's peculiar behavior and claimed the doll would change expressions when no one was looking and often move from room to room on its own.

One day, Robert declared that he should no longer be referred to as Robert, as that was the doll's name, and should instead be called Eugene. Not thinking too much of it and thinking it was likely a phase, those in Robert's— er, Eugene's—orbit obliged.

One of the more unsettling aspect of the story was the way the doll seemed to wield a malevolent influence over those around him. Visitors to the Otto household reported feeling an overwhelming sense of dread in the presence of the doll, and some even claimed to have seen him blink or heard him speak.

As Eugene grew older, Robert's hold over the Otto family only seemed to strengthen. Despite their best efforts to rid themselves of the doll—locking him away in the attic, throwing him out with the trash—he always found his way back, his piercing gaze and sinister smile a constant reminder of the darkness that lurked within. And every time something went wrong, and Eugene was disciplined, the familiar refrain: "Robert did it" could be heard.

Today, Robert the Doll resides in a glass case at the Fort East Martello Museum in Key West, where he continues to enamor visitors from around the world. Some say that if you look into his glass eyes for too long, you'll feel a chill run down your spine and hear his mischievous laughter echoing in your ears. Others say that if you spend enough time with him, you'll see him move. Still more say you should never take his picture without asking, as it will result in a curse. People from all over have written apologies to Robert after visiting the museum and taking his photo, only to return home to a series of bad luck and tragedy.

I didn't experience that when I visited, but I did feel something. And that night's paranormal investigation at the fort resulted in some compelling evidence. But the one thing I will tell you given my experience is that you should never ask for permission. That is just inviting the dark entity in and will cause more harm than good. But the part about being polite and not chastising the doll—or the legion of spirits thought to inhabit it? Yeah, definitely do that.

Robert's story is a cautionary tale about the dangers of playing with forces beyond our understanding and the troubling consequences that can follow when we dare to toy with the unknown.

THE GREAT BED OF WARE

Alrighty, let's embark on a tale of intrigue, grandeur,

and a bed so legendary it captured the hearts of generations. This is the story of the Great Bed of Ware, a marvel of craftsmanship and a relic of bygone days.

Our journey begins in the quaint English town of Ware, nestled in the rolling hills of Hertfordshire. It was here, in the late sixteenth century, that a master carpenter by the name of Jonas Fosbrooke set out to create a bed fit for royalty.

Legend has it that Fosbrooke crafted the Great Bed as a showpiece for his inn, The White Hart, hoping to attract wealthy travelers and nobility passing through the area. And what a showpiece it was! Standing over ten feet wide and eleven feet long, the bed was a sight to behold—a veritable fortress of wood and fabric, adorned with intricate carvings and luxurious draperies.

But the true magic of the Great Bed lay not in its size or its craftsmanship, but in the stories it inspired. Tales of star-crossed lovers, weary travelers, and scandalous liaisons whispered in the dimly lit halls of The White Hart, weaving a tapestry of intrigue and romance around the bed's towering frame.

As the years passed, the Great Bed became more than just a piece of furniture—it became a symbol of hospitality, luxury, and the timeless allure of the English countryside. Travelers from far and wide flocked to The White Hart to marvel at its splendor and perhaps even steal a glimpse of the secrets hidden within its massive embrace.

But like all good stories, the tale of the Great Bed of Ware is not without its mysteries. People say that it was once the resting place of kings and queens, and others claim that it was cursed by a jealous lover or haunted by restless spirits.

Whatever the truth may be, one thing is for certain—the Great Bed of Ware remains a testament to the enduring power of storytelling and the timeless appeal of a good night's sleep. So, the next time you find yourself in London, be sure to pay a visit to the V&A and see the bed that captured the hearts and imaginations of generations past. You might uncover some secrets within its grand and storied embrace.

Chapter Eleven

Time Travel and Parallel Universes

IN THE VAST tapestry of the cosmos, there exist realms beyond our comprehension, where the boundaries of time and space blur and the fabric of reality bends to the whims of the unknown. Welcome to the enigmatic domain of time travel and parallel universes, where the very essence of existence is called into question. In the sections that follow, we embark on a daring exploration of the mysteries that extend beyond the confines of conventional understanding. From the mind-bending paradoxes of temporal manipulation to the infinite possibilities of alternate dimensions, let us travel some of the uncharted courses of the universe and dare to confront the profound questions that have captivated the human imagination for centuries.

THE PHILADELPHIA EXPERIMENT

The Philadelphia Experiment holds strong as one of

the top and most intriguing, controversial paranormal occurrences in history. This mysterious event allegedly took place in 1943 during World War II, when the U.S. Navy conducted a secret experiment to render a warship invisible to enemy radar. According to reports, the U.S.S. Eldridge vanished from sight and reappeared moments later in a different location. The crew members were said to have experienced severe physical and mental side effects, including nausea, disorientation, and even teleportation.

Many skeptics dismiss the Philadelphia Experiment as a hoax or a myth, but there are those who believe that it actually happened. Some researchers claim that the experiment was based on the work of Nikola Tesla, a brilliant inventor and scientist who was known for his groundbreaking theories on energy and frequency. They suggest that the Navy used Tesla's ideas to create a device that could manipulate electromagnetic fields and bend space and time.

The alleged survivors of the Philadelphia Experiment have shared harrowing accounts of their experiences, claiming that they were caught in a nightmarish vortex of time and space. Some of them reported seeing strange beings and alien landscapes, while others claimed to have traveled to different dimensions. These stories have fueled speculation that the experiment had unintended consequences, opening a portal to other realms or alternate realities.

Despite lacking any true evidence, the Philadelphia Experiment still holds nearly all paranormal enthusiasts and conspiracy theorists in thrall. The mystery surrounding the event has inspired numerous books, documentaries, and even a Hollywood movie. Some believe that the experiment was part of a larger government conspiracy to harness supernatural powers for military purposes. Others view it as an advisory about the dangers of tampering with forces beyond our understanding.

Whether the Philadelphia Experiment was a real event or a clever hoax, its legacy lives on in the annals of paranormal history. The unanswered questions and unresolved mysteries surrounding the experiment serve as a reminder of the boundless possibilities of the unknown. As we immerse ourselves more in the realms of all things woo-woo and ancient mysteries, the truth behind the Philadelphia Experiment may someday come to light. Or, it could remain forever shrouded in secrecy.

THE MONTAUK PROJECT

The Montauk Project is another incredibly mysterious and controversial topic. This project is said to have taken place at Camp Hero in Montauk, New York, and has been linked to various conspiracy theories and supernatural occurrences. Many believe that the Montauk Project involved experiments in time travel, mind control, and even contact with extraterrestrial beings.

The origins of the Montauk Project are shrouded in secrecy, with some claiming that it was an extension of the infamous Philadelphia Experiment, where a U.S.

Navy destroyer was said to have been rendered invisible during World War II. According to some accounts, the Montauk Project was a continuation of these experiments, with a focus on manipulating time and space for military purposes. Others believe that the project was a cover for more sinister activities, such as mind control experiments on unwitting subjects.

One of the greatest aspects of the Montauk Project is that some claim the project involved harnessing the psychic abilities of individuals to create a powerful weapon or to communicate with other dimensions. Reports of telekinesis, telepathy, and remote viewing have all been linked to the Montauk Project, leading many to speculate about the true nature of the experiments that took place there.

All details of the Montauk Project continue to enrapture those in love with these kinds of mysteries. Some believe that the project may have uncovered hidden knowledge or artifacts that could rewrite history as we know it. Others speculate that the experiments conducted at Camp Hero may have inadvertently opened a portal to another realm, allowing for the presence of ghosts, aliens, or other supernatural entities to manifest in the area.

Overall, the Montauk Project remains a wonder-filled and enigmatic chapter in the annals of paranormal research. Whether it was a government cover-up, a scientific breakthrough, or something even more sinister, the truth behind the Montauk Project may never be fully known, leaving us to wonder about the secrets that lie hidden in the shadows of history.

. . .

THE MANDELA EFFECT

The Mandela Effect is a attention-grabbing phenomenon. Named after former South African president Nelson Mandela, this strange occurrence refers to the collective misremembering of certain events or details. For example, some people swear they remember Nelson Mandela dying in prison in the 1980s, even though he actually passed away in 2013. This has led some to speculate that there may be alternate realities or timelines at play.

One of the best examples of the Mandela Effect is the children's book series, *The Berenstain Bears*. Many people remember the title as *The Berenstein Bears*, with an "e" instead of an "a." This discrepancy has sparked countless debates online, with some attributing it to a glitch in the matrix or even evidence of time travel.

Some believe that certain individuals possess the ability to shift between parallel universes, causing discrepancies in collective memory. This has led to the theory that those experiencing the Mandela Effect may be more in tune with the supernatural world than others.

Ancient mysteries and archaeological anomalies have also been tied to the Mandela Effect. Some researchers believe that artifacts from past civilizations may hold clues to understanding the phenomenon. For example, ancient texts and hieroglyphics depicting events that contradict known history could be evidence of alternate timelines intersecting with our own.

Overall, the Mandela Effect remains an alluring

mystery that forever puzzles and intrigues those with an interest in the paranormal. Whether it is a simple case of false memory or something more otherworldly, this phenomenon is just one more piece of the puzzle in the vast tapestry of the unknown.

JOHN TITOR

The story of John Titor sparks widespread fascination and debate among conspiracy theorists and armchair detectives alike.

It all began in the year 2000, when a mysterious figure going by the pseudonym John Titor appeared on various online forums, claiming to be a time traveler from the year 2036. According to Titor, he had been sent back in time to retrieve a vintage computer necessary to repair a malfunctioning future world.

Over the course of several months, John Titor engaged in discussions with curious internet users, sharing detailed descriptions of his supposed future world, including predictions about geopolitical events, technological advancements, and even warnings about impending societal collapse.

One of the more riveting aspects of John Titor's story was his detailed explanation of time travel mechanics, including discussions about the concept of diverging timelines and the potential for alternate realities. According to Titor, his journey back to the past had created a new timeline, separate from the one he had left behind.

As word of John Titor's claims spread, he gained a

cult following, with many people captivated by his apparent insights into the future. However, skepticism abounded, with critics pointing out inconsistencies in Titor's story and questioning the feasibility of his alleged time travel exploits.

Eventually, John Titor disappeared from the internet as mysteriously as he had arrived, leaving a legacy shrouded in uncertainty and speculation in his wake. His true identity remains unknown, confounding those who've searched for answers, and the question of whether he was a genuine time traveler or an elaborate prankster lives on, continuing to divide opinion.

Regardless of the veracity of his claims, the story of John Titor remains a interesting example of the power of internet mythology and the enduring allure of the unknown. Whether he was a messenger from the future or merely a skilled storyteller, his legacy lives on as a testament to the boundless imagination of the human spirit.

NOAH

No, not that Noah. This Noah emerged on the internet in 2017, captivating audiences with his tantalizing claims of time travel and apocalyptic visions.

According to "Noah," he was a time traveler from the year 2030 who had been sent back to the past to warn humanity about impending cataclysms and societal upheavals. Through a series of cryptic YouTube videos and online posts, Noah shared his predictions about future events, ranging from technological advancements to global conflicts and environmental disasters.

One of the best and most intriguing aspects of Noah's story was his alleged possession of a device known as the "Noah Time Traveler's Box," which he claimed allowed him to communicate across time and space. Noah described using this device to send messages to his future self and to access information from his own timeline.

As Noah's story gained traction online, it sparked intense speculation and debate among internet users, with some people believing him to be a genuine time traveler and others dismissing him as a hoaxer or attention seeker. Skeptics pointed to inconsistencies in Noah's story and questioned the lack of concrete evidence to support his claims.

Despite the controversy surrounding his identity and motives, Noah's story captured the interest of many, tapping into the timeless fascination with the concept of time travel and the unknown of the future. Regardless of whether he was a skilled storyteller spinning elaborate tales, the legend of Noah from 2017 endures, sparking and rousing curiosity to this day.

YEAR 5000 PHOTO

What kind of evidence would you accept from a time traveler? Well, in 2018, a man named Edward claimed to have traveled to the year 5000 and returned with photographic proof. He asserted that he was selected in 2004 for a secret project which sent him into the future. According to him, the photo he shared of an underwater city is actually Los Angeles three thousand years in the future. By that time, the world will presumably have been flooded by global warming and mankind will survive by living in floating cities—like the one in the photo he took. I know it's sounds far-fetched, but you have to admit you're wondering whether or not our future will be like *Waterworld*.

Chapter Twelve

Exploring the Unknown

THE FUTURE OF PARANORMAL RESEARCH

As we look toward the future of paranormal research, it is important to consider the advancements that have been made in recent years. With technology constantly evolving, researchers now have access to tools and equipment that were once unimaginable. This has allowed for a more in-depth exploration of the supernatural world, uncovering new mysteries and phenomena that were previously unknown.

One exciting area of paranormal research that is gaining traction is the study of psychic *powers*. Through the use of mediums, psychics, and other gifted individuals, researchers are able to delve deeper into inner workings of the mind and explore the limits of human potential. These studies have led to wonderful discoveries that challenge our perception.

Another intriguing aspect of the growing field of paranormal research is the exploration of ancient mysteries and archaeological anomalies. By studying ancient civilizations and their beliefs in the supernatural, researchers are able to gain valuable insights into the history of paranormal occurrences. From the pyramids of Egypt to the ruins of Machu Picchu, these ancient sites hold clues to the mysteries of the past and offer a glimpse into the supernatural world.

For those of us who love this stuff, it is crucial to support and engage with the ongoing research in these fields. By staying informed and open-minded, we can contribute to the advancement of paranormal research and help uncover the truths behind things just out of our reach. The future holds endless possibilities, and by coming together as a community, we can continue to push the boundaries of what is known and explore the mysteries that lie beyond.

While paranormal research has historically been viewed with skepticism by the scientific community, there has been a growing interest in exploring these phenomena using rigorous scientific methods. Here are some academic examples of the direction the coming decades of paranormal research is heading:

1. Interdisciplinary Approaches: Many researchers are adopting interdisciplinary approaches that draw on insights from fields such as psychology, neuroscience, physics, and anthropology to study paranormal phenomena. By integrating knowledge from multiple disciplines, researchers aim to develop more comprehensive theories and

methodologies for investigating paranormal experiences.

2. Experimental Studies: There is a growing emphasis on conducting experimental studies to test hypotheses related to paranormal phenomena. For example, researchers may use controlled laboratory experiments to investigate extrasensory perception (ESP), telekinesis, or remote viewing. These studies often involve rigorous experimental designs, randomization, and statistical analysis to ensure the validity and reliability of the findings.

3. Quantitative Analysis: Advances in data analytics and computational methods have enabled researchers to analyze large datasets related to paranormal experiences. For example, researchers may use quantitative analysis techniques to examine patterns in reported sightings of UFOs or analyze trends in near-death experiences. By applying quantitative methods, researchers can identify correlations, trends, and anomalies that may provide insights into the nature of paranormal phenomena.

4. Field Studies: Some researchers are conducting field studies in real-world settings to investigate reported cases of hauntings, poltergeist activity, or other paranormal phenomena. These studies often involve careful observation, documentation, and

analysis of eyewitness accounts, physical evidence, and environmental factors. By conducting field studies, researchers aim to gain a better understanding of the cultural, social, and environmental factors that may contribute to paranormal experiences.

5. Technological Innovations: Advances in technology, such as electromagnetic field (EMF) detectors, thermal imaging cameras, and audio recording devices, are enabling researchers to collect more sophisticated data related to paranormal phenomena. Researchers are also exploring the use of emerging technologies, such as virtual reality (VR) and augmented reality (AR), to simulate paranormal experiences in controlled laboratory settings or investigate the psychological mechanisms underlying paranormal beliefs.

Overall, the future of paranormal research is characterized by a commitment to scientific rigor, interdisciplinary collaboration, and the application of advanced technologies and methodologies. By adopting a systematic and evidence-based approach, researchers aim to shed light on the hidden depths of the paranormal and contribute to our understanding of the human experience.

All in all, the future is bright and promising. With advancements in technology and a growing interest in the supernatural, researchers are making significant strides in unraveling the tangled web that is the mystery of the unknown. By embracing these discoveries and supporting ongoing research, we can continue to expand our understanding of the paranormal world and unlock the secrets of the past. As we look ahead to the future, let us remain curious, open- minded, and dedicated to exploring the realms of the supernatural.

Take me, for example. I am currently in the process of getting my PhD in Paranormal Sciences from Thomas Francis University and it is endlessly fascinating. The doctorate may not be accepted by academics, but it is a real and legal degree, and I am loving every minute of learning new things.

So, stay curious, stay weird, and remember...the truth is out there.

Also Available from Rayvn Salvador

Return to Hell: A Haunted New Orleans World Standalone

Behind the Veil: A Haunted New Orleans Special

ALSO ON THE WAY...

<u>The Lagniappe Isle Series – a Haunted New Orleans Spin-off:</u>

Art de la Morte

Esprit de la Lune

Le Feu Follet

About the Author

About Rayvn Salvador

New York Times and *USA Today* bestselling author Rayvn Salvador is a lifelong bibliophile who left her eighteen-year IT career over a decade ago to read and make stuff up for a living. She lives in Florida with her feline familiars and incredibly supportive beau—who hopes nobody ever needs to check her search history. They love to attend sporting events and concerts, but if she's not doing that and isn't on deadline, you'll likely find her taking long walks through the woods, sweating while working out in virtual reality, investigating haunted locales, or contemplating the recesses of people's minds in documentaries. She currently pens the Haunted New Orleans (paranormal romantic thriller), Willow Falls (small-town romantic suspense) and Fourth and Goal (football romance) series, and is hard at work on the next book to make your pulse race.

Stay Connected

Stay Connected

You can find Rayvn in all the usual bookish places...

Website: http://rayvnsalvador.com

Facebook: https://www.facebook.com/RayvnSalvador

Instagram: https://www.instagram.com/rayvnsalvador/

Goodreads: https://bit.ly/3ch4awz

BookBub: https://www.bookbub.com/profile/rayvn-salvador

Amazon: https://amzn.to/2TUXE0R

Twitter: https://twitter.com/RayvnSalvador

Praise for Rayvn Salvador

Praise for Rayvn Salvador

"Rich with New Orleans history, this entry will delight fans of paranormal romance. An EDITOR'S PICK."

~Publisher's Weekly Booklife

"An often-engaging paranormal tale with spice and scares."

~Kirkus Reviews

"Spooky, addictive, and sexy as hell, Ms. Salvador knows how to write a page-turner!"

~NY Times bestselling author Darynda Jones

"Gripping, sensual, and captivating. I was hooked from the first page of this compelling love story."

~NY Times bestselling author Donna Grant

"Ghosts, mysteries, romance, New Orleans, and a serial killer—Memento Mori is a perfect read!"

~*USA Today* Bestselling Author Angela Roquet

"Rayvn Salvador pens an exhilarating and romantic tale you don't want to miss!"

~*USA Today* Bestselling Author Jen Talty

"An exciting author!"

~*USA Today* Bestselling Author Michele Hauf

"Words that bring vivid imagery, along with swoon-worthy feels."

~*USA Today* Bestselling Author Tigris Eden/J.K. Rivers

"[Haunted New Orleans] is a beautiful gumbo of romance, mystery, magic, ghosts, voodoo, and love beyond the grave."

~5-Star Reviewer

"First of all, it seems like this amazing author is a descriptive genius since I truly felt like I was in New Orleans, and the paranormal aspect of it really gave me goosebumps at the end of the day, so it's safe to say that I didn't just read it, I experienced every moment."

~5-Star Reviewer

"Rayvn puts so much history into her Haunted New Orleans series. You feel like if these places really exist, their stories are true."

Praise for Rayvn Salvador

~5-Star Reviewer

Made in the USA
Middletown, DE
07 April 2024